ROBERT *the* BRUCE's
FORGOTTEN VICTORY

ROBERT *the* BRUCE's
FORGOTTEN VICTORY

The Battle of Byland 1322

GRAHAM BELL

TEMPUS

First published 2005

Tempus Publishing Limited
The Mill, Brimscombe Port,
Stroud, Gloucestershire, GL5 2QG
www.tempus-publishing.com

British Library Cataloguing in Publication Data.
A catalogue record for this book is available from the British Library.

ISBN 0 7524 3323 7

Typesetting and origination by Tempus Publishing Limited
Printed in Great Britain

Contents

About the Author

G raham Bell is the author of *Yorkshire Battlefields: A Guide to the Great Conflicts on Yorkshire Soil 937–1461* and *Famous Yorkshire Deaths*. He has an MA in War Studies from King's College, London and lives in Sheffield.

Preface

In October 1322, on a ridge in Yorkshire, two kings of adjacent areas of Britain faced each other to do battle. It would be the second time the two had met. On the first occasion, one had inflicted on the other the most disastrous defeat suffered by the loser's kingdom for two-and-a-half centuries; the result of the second encounter would be the same. The difference was that on the second occasion the humiliation suffered by the loser would be one step towards an appallingly brutal and sadistic death in Berkeley Castle; for the other, it would be perhaps the apogee of his kingship and skill as a military commander. This is the story of the battle of Byland.

Unlike the battle of Bannockburn, which (despite the remarks of some of the more cynical historians) in effect ensured Scottish independence, the battle of Byland is unknown even to many of the scholars of the fourteenth century. It had, however, as much treachery, anger and violence as any combat of the age, and allowed the victor, Robert the Bruce, to show skill and daring the like of which can only be compared to the heroism shown by King Harold in 1066, and which would lead to the loser, Edward II, being described by his own people as chicken-hearted and luckless.

The story begins, as most good thrillers do, on a dark night, in a place where the stormy seas lashed the seashore, when all respectable people were in bed. It begins in Scotland in 1289...

Introduction

So utterly vile was the weather in Scotland on the night of 18 March 1286, according to the Lanercost chronicler, that most citizens stayed in their houses. In Edinburgh, King Alexander III of the Scots was attending a meeting of his council. There was a rumour that soon it would be Judgement Day, and that the world would end. Alexander, like most kings, paid very little attention to such absurd ideas, and sent a platter of food to one of his earls, telling him to be merry, as the day of judgement was at hand. The earl replied in the same spirit that if it were, they would meet it with full bellies.

The council appeared to end on this jolly note, and the king took it upon himself to leave the city and cross the Firth of Forth, the stretch of sea to the north of Edinburgh, and visit his wife. He had married Yolande de Dreux only recently and, most inconveniently, she was lodged at Kinghorn, on a rather remote stretch of the Fife coastline, separated from her lord and master by a stormy sea and three miles of rough tracks.

His council tried to stop him on this errand, since the waters of the Forth were stormy, and the road to the house where the queen of the Scots lodged was dangerous (as any road would be on a pitch-black and stormy night). The king, however, overruled his council, deciding to cross over the Forth and perform his conjugal duties, the main duty of a king in the fourteenth century, of course, being to beget healthy and strong heirs.

At the water's edge, the ferryman urged him to turn back, saying these nocturnal duties would be the death of him. Alexander, with the kingly knack of shaming his subjects into doing his bidding, overruled advice for the second time and set out to visit his queen, who, judging by the risks he was running, must have been a most delectable morsel indeed. On reaching the north shore of the Forth, in the ancient earldom of Fife, the king set out on horseback to Kinghorn. Given the darkness of the night, and the near gale-force winds now raging, it is not surprising that he soon became separated from his guides. It is even less surprising that on the following morning the king's body was found at the bottom of the cliffs: he had plunged to his death in the night.

This moment of lust and impatience would lead to a series of wars which would go on intermittently for over three centuries, and would only end when the two kingdoms of England and Scotland were united in 1603 by that most unappealing and incompetent creature, James I of England.

I

Scotland: People of Ireland?

The battle of Byland, like all battles, has its antecedents in the history of the armies that fought it. About 500 years after the birth of Christ, Scotland was inhabited by a people described generically as Picts. They left little behind them to tell us of what they were really like, except impressive stone towers and tombs, indecipherable symbols they carved onto stone pillars, and a reputation for savagery and for painting themselves in blue paint.

In about the year AD 560, a group of invaders from Ireland left their home, believed to have been in the county of Armagh, and sailed the short distance east, landing on the west coast of Scotland in modern-day Argyll. Their leader was called Fergus Mac Erc, and they brought with them very little to differentiate them from the Picts (both being Celtic peoples) except for a piece of baggage called the Lia Fiall, or the Stone of Destiny. This was supposed to be the stone on which the ancient prophet Jacob had slept, which had been transported to Scotland in the travels of the Scots via Spain and Ireland.

The Scots and the Picts seem to have lived together in perfect equanimity, an equanimity that was only temporarily interrupted when the Christians made their appearance in Alba (as the ancient kingdom of Scotland was known). The man who converted the Picts and the Scots to Christianity was Columba, an Irish prince who had to make, it appears, a fairly hurried exit from Ireland in about AD 563. By the time of his death in AD 597, the whole of the land had become Christian (according to later historians), and the Isle of Iona on the west coast of Scotland had become the official burial place of the king of the Scots.

We now come to a rather strange occurrence in the history of Scotland. It is known that in AD 843 the king of the Scots, Kenneth Mcalpin, became king of the Picts, most likely through being elected by the Mormaors of Scotland. These men were the great officers of the various areas of the lands of the Picts, who would later be called the Earls of Scotland. They were the Lords of Fife (in later days considered to be the premier area of Scotland), Stratherarn, Angus, Mar, Moray, Ross and Caithness.

Why Kenneth was elected to be the overlord of his Pictish neighbours is something of a mystery. Some have pointed out that at about this time Scotland, like the rest of Christendom, began to be bitterly affected by increasing raids from the Vikings, who were now becoming the terror of the west. Kenneth was a successful warrior, and a good warrior was needed at the helm, especially as the Vikings killed at least two Pictish kings at this time. Suffice to say, Kenneth became king of the Scots and appeared to rule well (which in those days meant being successful in battle), and the line of kings of Scotland would now be called Macalpin for generations.

The next few hundred years followed the pattern of most Christian kingdoms on the continent – in other words, a tale of slaughter and bloodshed as the various kings and Mormaors fought with each other, and sometimes with the Vikings.

It should be pointed out that the orbit of the kingdom was almost entirely to the north of the Firth of Forth, which until well into the thirteenth century was called the Scottish Sea. The land south of the Forth, though originally inhabited by Picts, was now inhabited by a tribe of the Angles who, with their cousins the Jutes and Saxons, had invaded the British mainland in the fifth century. It was these people who would be the most dangerous foes the Scots would ever encounter, and who would to all intents and purposes overwhelm them. As the Picts had rallied under Kenneth Mcalpin, so the peoples of the south rallied under Alfred the Great, the king of Wessex, perhaps the greatest ruler these isles have ever known. By defeating the invading Vikings, and expanding his kingdom to the north, Alfred's line not only became kings of Wessex, but kings of England.

As Alfred had started the West-Saxon kingdom, the most southerly of the British kingdoms, on its march to greatness, his heirs began to absorb the kingdoms to the north, which had ominous implications for the Scots. Alfred's grandson, Athelstan the Magnificent, showed the power of the Saxons by leading a huge raid into the heartland of the Scots in AD 934.

Alarmed at this humiliation, the king of the Scots, Constantine III, raised a huge coalition of Scotsmen, northern Britons and pirates called in for the plunder, and marched down to smash this threat to the independence of the north. At a place called Brunanburgh, most likely near Sheffield, his army was routed by Athelstan in the greatest victory in the history of the old Anglo-Saxons. Constantine wisely rejected any further ideas about attacking his southern neighbours, and for the next few decades relative peace reigned over the border between the Scots and the Anglo-Saxons. It must once again be noted that 'Scotland', in this context, refers to the area above the line of the Forth, the area between the Forth and the Tweed being a sort of no-man's-land ruled by whichever sword-wielding thug happened to be top of the heap at that time. The history of this area, together with the whole of the islands of Britain, would be changed in the year 1066.

The ruler of the kingdom of the Scots at this time was a noticeably vile individual by the name of Malcolm Canmore, famous mostly for being the king in Shakespeare who overthrew the tyrant Macbeth and brought an age of peace and prosperity to the lands of the north. It is now generally recognised that Macbeth was regarded as a humane and intelligent man, under whose reign Scotland reached a peak of prosperity never before seen. It is also recognised that Malcolm was, even by the standards of the time, a vicious and savage boor whose reputation as a noble king was invented almost at the command of James I of England.

Malcolm may have been visited in this year by the former Earl of Northumbria, Tostig, who had been exiled from his lands as a result of his savage quelling of the laws of the Northumbrians. Enraged at this treatment, he sailed to Norway to enlist the help of Harold of Norway, the most famous psychopath of the age, to regain his lands. If he did so, any advice or help he may have received from Malcolm was in vain, since at Stamford Bridge Harold and Tostig were surprised by Tostig's brother, Harold of England, in perhaps the greatest military manoeuvre in the history of the Saxon kingdom, and were slaughtered together with most of their men.

This victory was to prove a bitterly short triumph for the heroic Harold, since almost at the same time as he was fighting his treacherous brother, William, Duke of the Normans (who, with Henry V, was one of the most sadistic and evil men ever to rule England) landed unopposed in the south of England. Harold, over-confident as a result of his earlier victory, hurried south to meet William. At the bloody field at Senlac, Harold of England, facing an enemy which outnumbered him and a man who was a much more subtle general than Hardrada, died, fighting for his kingdom with his housecarles around him. With his death, a new and more ruthless method of administration would enter Britain: the feudal system. It would eventually affect not only England, but also Scotland.

Malcolm's initial response to this change of affairs in the south was to launch a series of vicious invasions of Northumbria, which only ended in 1072 when William, having slaughtered a large part of the Saxon population of England, swept north to invade Scotland by both land and sea. Malcolm, who added realism to his savagery, realised that he was between a rock and a hard place, and placated William at the River Tay by agreeing to become his vassal. William, having more important things to do than slaughter some savages to the north of his kingdom, went home; Malcolm promptly forgot about the oath, and continued raiding Northumbria.

At almost the same time as William marched to Scotland, a ship sailing away from England was washed up on the coast of Northumbria. This ship had a very interesting cargo: the sons and daughters of the old royal house of Wessex, now fleeing, as a large part of the English people were, from the savagery of William of Normandy. One of them, the half-Hungarian Margaret, appears to have overwhelmed Malcolm by her beauty and strength of character. She was sent back to Scotland as a semi-prisoner; Malcolm, after taking the precaution of poisoning his current wife, married Margaret, with dire results for the future of the Scots.

2

The Margaretsons and the Coming of the Saxons

The reign of Malcolm Canmore is so closely linked to his marriage with Margaret, the half-Hungarian Saxon princess he married in such ambiguous circumstances, that their children have been known by historians as the Margaretsons ever since.

This matronymic is a symbol of how Margaret would change the way Scotland was ruled and administered. Shaking off whatever feelings she had about her enforced incarceration, she proceeded to take a hand in the running of the kingdom of the Scots in a way that no other woman had done before. In true medieval fashion, she encouraged trade and manufacture. She was also, it seems, very generous to the poor and tried to improve the conditions of the serfs and peasants. The serf population had increased fairly drastically in the years of Malcolm's reign, since (in complete violation of his oath to William) Malcolm kept raiding Northumbria, with the result that the slaves and refugees unexpectedly brought to the northlands were so numerous that the English language began to dominate the area between the Forth and the Tweed, eventually wiping out the Gaelic tongue in that area.

As well as indulging in these all-too-praiseworthy acts, Margaret, in a movement which may have been more a reaction to her unhappy family life than a true vocation, tried, with a great deal of success,

to reform the old Celtic Church. She objected to many of its prac-
tices: its habit of holding open-air services; the way the Celtic priests
shaved their hair on the forehead and not on the crown; the fact that
the Celtic priests wore only homespun habits and not the beautiful
vestments favoured by the Catholic clergy. Margaret's sense of order
must also have been offended by the fact that there did not seem to
be any form of order in the ecclesiastical ranks of the old Church.

Margaret went ahead with her reforms, building stone churches
(which of course were then tenanted by Romish priests) and changing the way Easter was celebrated in Scotland. The fact that she
succeeded in most of what she set out to do was due in no small
part to the fact that, as queen of the Scots, wife of a man who would
not hesitate to murder to get his own way, her suggestions had some
force behind them. She must have had some emotional hold over her
savage husband, as evidenced by the fact that her sons were all given
distinctly un-Gaelic names. In chronological order, they were called
Edward, Ethelred, Edmund, Edgar, Alexander and David. The three
sons of Malcolm's first marriage had been efficiently dealt with: the
eldest, Duncan, was held as a hostage at the court of Malcolm's fel-
low savage, William the Conqueror, and the other two were sent into
exile in the highland wastes of the north.

Punishment for the cruelties he had inflicted on the earldom of
Northumbria visited Malcolm with a vengeance in 1093. Raiding
the March, he was killed in an ambush near Alnmouth. To make
things worse for the Scots, and for Margaret personally, her eldest
son Edward was also badly wounded in the raid, and died on the way
home to Scotland, at Jedburgh.

This double blow of family tragedy shattered Margaret, who,
according to some accounts, was suffering a crisis of conscience
about her treatment of the old Church of Columba. She had been
quietly starving herself for a long time, and going on exhausting
penances in order to show her piety. On the news of her husband's
and son's deaths, she herself died, a broken woman, in St Margaret's
Chapel in Edinburgh.

It was probably a good thing that Margaret died when she did. Donald Ban, the brother of Malcolm, who had spent his life in the northern fastness, came south and, with the agreement of the Mormaors of the realm (for convenience's sake we shall now call them earls), was elected king. The sons and daughters of Margaret (apart from Edmund, now a priest in a Roman Catholic monastery, and Ethelred, who to his mother's consternation had gone native, become a priest of the Celtic Church, and actually changed his name to the rather less euphonious Eth) fled to the court of William I's son, the roistering rogue William Rufus. Rufus, eager to show that he was his father's son, almost immediately placed the half-forgotten Duncan, much-abused son of Malcolm IV's first wife, at the head of an army and sent him to overthrow the Gaelic trouble-maker.

Duncan appears to have defeated his uncle with surprising ease. In a gesture of goodwill, which just goes to show that good men do not usually finish first, he sent home his English army (in reality a Norman/Saxon army) to show he could rule without them, trusting in the love of his long-lost Scottish subjects. Donald Ban was soon back on the throne, after Duncan's inevitable murder at Mondynes, in the Mearns.

The reign of this last true Celtic king was a short one: in 1097, Rufus, free from fighting in Normandy, sent another army to Scotland which, under the command of Edgar, the fourth Margaretson, over-threw Donald. Edgar was not going to make the same mistake as his brother. Having captured Donald Ban, he ordered his eyes to be put out. To add insult to injury, he then had his wretched uncle work as a scullion in the royal kitchens.

The first of the Margaretsons to wear a crown, Edgar proved to be a solemn, reclusive character of whom little is known, and none of that particularly interesting. When he died in 1107, there was a general feeling of relief, and his brother Alexander, the second of the Margaretsons, took over. Alexander, unlike his brother, enjoyed wine, women and song; he was hot-tempered and lacked judgement, but really had very little to deal with during his reign. The current Norman king of England, Henry I, proved to be fully occupied with maintaining his position as king of the southern realm, following the probable murder of his brother, William Rufus, in 1100.

There was a notable lack of tension between the kingdoms of Scotland and England at this time. Little occurred in the way of wars and raiding, a fact which caused much distress to bloody-minded scholars of the Victorian period; Alexander married one of Henry I's apparently limitless supply of bastards; and, most importantly, Alexander's brother David, the youngest of the Margaretsons, was appointed governor of Cumbria.

3

David and the Coming of the Normans

The battle of Byland, the Scottish Wars of Independence, and the story of the Wallace, the Bruce and Edward Longshanks, are directly related to the reforms and laws that David brought to the kingdom of the Scots. David had followed his family into exile when the unfortunate Donald Ban was proclaimed king for the first time in 1093. As a royal prince, he would most likely have been treated with some respect and deference. It is quite clear that he spent a lot of time studying and observing the strict Anglo-Saxon and Norman administrations of England while he was there. He was given a good education, something he made full use of when his brother-in-law, Henry of England, in typically shrewd fashion, solved what was seemingly an insoluble problem.

As has been mentioned already, the old kingdom of the Scots was to be found north of the Forth and Clyde; it was only recently that the Scottish kings had started living in Edinburgh, in the Lothian. To the west and south-west of this area were the lands of Galloway and Cumbria. At the time of the Saxon Athelstan, all of this area, from Dumbarton near Loch Lomond down the west of modern Scotland and almost to Lancaster in England, was part of the old Dark Age kingdom of Strathclyde.

By the twelfth century this rather bizarre kingdom had broken up, and Cumbria and Galloway had become completely independent in everything but name. They were known for their ferocity and for their lack of loyalty to anyone who tried to rule them. Henry I, like a true Norman always on the look-out for fresh lands to conquer, saw in Cumbria a fertile field for expansion. But how could he dominate an area so close to the land of Alexander, without the tedium of having to fight a war with his northern neighbour?

With the shrewdness that was to be a hallmark of his reign, Henry came up with a solution which, like all great ideas, was very simple: he would make David, Alexander's brother, governor of Cumbria. Henry considered, quite rightly, that Alexander would not object to his own brother being put in a position of responsibility, if not on his doorstep, at least near his own front gate. Furthermore, as the Cumbrians and the Gallowegians had never shown a desire to be ruled by anybody (and certainly not by their northern neighbours), Alexander could only wish his brother luck in taking over such a troublesome land.

In 1112, therefore, David, the last and ultimately the most able and likeable of the Margaretsons, rode north to take over his inheritance. This date should be marked in Scotland's schoolrooms with as much importance as 1314, when the Bruce emerged victorious at Bannockburn, and 1746, when Bonnie Prince Charlie was defeated by the Duke of Cumberland at Culloden.

4

David and the Making of Medieval Scotland

Having taken over the lands of Cumbria, and made his headquarters in Carlisle, a city which would later be his preferred place of residence, David soon found out that he was going to be given yet more responsibility. In a gesture which seemed to show that Alexander and Henry had been consulting on this matter for some time, Alexander made his brother governor of Scotland south of the Forth. The handing over of the administration of this land seems to show as much a lack of interest in the area by the fifth Margaretson as any deep family feeling; Alexander was more concerned with drinking, Highland games and wenching than ruling his lands.

Whatever the reasons, David found himself ruler of almost all of modern Scotland south of the Forth, and he promptly showed how much he had learned at the court of the Norman kings through the reforms he began to implement and the men he brought with him. Henry, realising that a ruler without force to back him up is like a scabbard without a sword, determined not to make the mistake Duncan had made when he became king of the Scots, and sent David to the north with a powerful bodyguard.

The men who came with David and who later followed him to the north, the land-hungry Norman lords, would later dominate the land of the Scots, and the names of the descendants of these Norman-French-speaking foreigners resonate throughout the chronicles for centuries. Although a few Norman families had come to Scotland in the reign of Alexander, the true Norman influence on the land of the Scots began with the coming of the youngest of the Margaretsons. The Lindsays and Urquharts, Gordons and Chisholms, Melvilles and Frasers all began to make their names in Scottish affairs at this time. Three other families whose descendants, for good or ill, would change the history of the land of the Scots also came to prominence at this time: the Bruces, Cummings (or Comyns) and Balliols.

With a powerful set of mounted and armoured knights behind him, David was able to start reforming the lands under his control. He had another advantage, which would prove to be even more important: a very, very rich wife. Before he came to Scotland, he had married Matilda, Countess of Northampton and Huntingdon. This meant he had as a wife a woman whose lands stretched across the English midlands, and whose revenues accordingly were huge. With her money, David proceeded to go on an administrative and building spree unsurpassed in Scotland until the Industrial Revolution. He rapidly changed the environment of the area he had taken over. To run an efficient administration, he of course needed a literate and trained civil service. In the twelfth century, the administration of the kingdoms of Europe was becoming much more sophisticated, and there was an increasing demand for learned men, educated in finance and the law. It was for this reason that David proceeded to build churches throughout Scotland, which also meant that he was building schools. The churches at Melrose, Dryburgh, Selkirk, Roxburgh and St Andrews all had their origins in David's drive to produce an educated elite, able to rule the land under his control.

He also needed a rational system of government. He proceeded to divide the lands under his rule into parishes, thousands of them, which had the advantage of reducing the power of the earls of the land. By supplying the parishes with an educated workforce (which of course came from the newly built churches), he created a group of

civil servants who owed their appointment to the crown, thus ensuring their loyalty. In 1123, Alexander died, and David, Earl of Carlisle,
became David I, king of the Scots – the last of the Margaretsons to
reach the throne.

An efficient administration required powerful civil servants, and
the youngest of the Margeretsons obtained these in a way which
showed how carefully he had observed the running of the lands to
the south. Instead of slaughtering the people over whom he ruled,
like the Williams of Normandy, David's Norman assistants took over
the lands of the Scots by the simple expedient of marrying heiresses,
or receiving lands from the royal domain. In this way, David got his
young friends into positions of responsibility in much the same way
as he himself had taken over Cumbria.

It is worth noting that, although there is general (and thoroughly justified) criticism of the way the Normans took over England,
owing to the policy of genocide used by William I, there has never
been anything like the same degree of controversy regarding the
Norman domination of Scotland. This seems to show that either
David had exceptional force of character (and, more importantly, the
manpower and cash to back up his reforms), or that the Norman
takeover was adopted with some enthusiasm by nearly all the members of the kingdom of the Scots, or that the reforms carried out by
David affected the rich to a quite disproportionate degree, and their
tenants and vassals merely went on as before, unnoticed and unimportant.

David also brought into Scotland something which had been on
the continent for over two centuries, and had been introduced to
England in 1066: the stone castle, synonymous with tales of der-
ring-do for centuries. The building of a castle, with its walls and
citadel made of stone, was a very lengthy and expensive affair. (Once
again, Matilda's dowry must have come in very useful here.) The
old Picts and Scots had been content with 'duns', which were resi-
dential forts, usually erected on strong defensive sites, but consisting
only of a rampart – a ditch of earth and turf surrounding a timber

stockade, within which were some simple huts and also the larger timber houses of the chiefs and richer men of the community. The residents lived and worked within the social and domestic confines they had known all their lives.

The Normans changed that: the castles that would soon extend from the Tweed to Inverness, and the Solway Firth to Aberdeen, were extremely visible tokens of the owners' intention of staying were they were. The castle was not only a symbol of might, and what would be called nowadays a sign of conspicuous consumption, but was the local administrative unit of the area in which it was situated – a storehouse during times of war, and a place of refuge for anyone lucky enough to be within its walls when an obstreperous neighbour attacked. A Scottish farmer who went inside a castle to pay his rents, or assist in a law case, would know that by entering the precincts of the Norman domain he was now part of a society in transition. The old patriarchal feeling believed to exist in the Scottish clan system (which may have been greatly exaggerated by romantics of the Victorian age) was to be substituted for a much more ruthless and merciless system of land ownership.

Despite these great social changes, it is generally assumed that David's reign was a great success: by bringing in a new political system, without destroying too much of the old one, David managed to bring to Scotland a peace which had not been seen for decades. The encouragement of trade and industry, in which the churches he helped build were of great importance, helped develop the medieval economy; in short, with the exception of one rather large glitch, David was by far the most successful of the Scottish medieval kings – perhaps the most important individual in Scottish history until the time the nation's destiny would be counted by the coal and iron ore to be found under its earth, rather than the number of its citizens.

One of the reasons David was able to make such great changes in Scotland is that, up until 1135, England was ruled by his cunning and cautious brother-in-law, Henry I. Since Henry had no desire to get himself embroiled in a northern war while he was busily consolidating his position in England, conquering Normandy and fighting his de jure sovereign, the king of France, the relations between the kingdoms of Scotland and England were, by medieval standards, exceptionally harmonious.

Henry's death in 1135, from over-indulgence in a meal of lampreys, threw everything into confusion. The English barons had to choose whether they would recognise Matilda, Henry's very arrogant and foolhardy daughter, as queen, or elect one of their own to be monarch. Their decision was rendered superfluous by the virtual *coup d'état* carried out by Henry's nephew, Stephen. It was very soon realised, however, that Stephen was not of the stuff of which medieval kings were made – meaning that he took no pleasure in the eye-gouging, hanging and mutilation carried out with such gusto by his overbearing uncle. Within a matter of weeks, rebellions broke out, and Stephen would be doomed for much of his reign to a heart-breaking trudge throughout the kingdom, trying to put down the barons who revolted against him.

The volatile situation in England made David decide to launch a series of raids soon after Stephen's accession. David claimed he was trying to help his niece, the Empress Matilda, become the rightful queen of England. Most observers think that, like any medieval king worth his salt, David was trying to grab whatever land was nearest to him. Whatever the reason, he launched a huge invasion of England in 1138 which would end in the most shattering defeat of his career.

At this point, it may be useful to examine what war meant to the people of the twelfth century, and to see how the reforms of David Margaretson had not only changed how people lived and ruled, but also how they killed each other.

5

The Rise of the Feudal Knight and the Growth of Fortifications

The collapse of the Roman Empire in the west, in the fifth century AD, had resulted in the creation of Dark Age kingdoms such as those of the Franks and Burgundians in continental Europe, and that of the Anglo-Saxons in England. They fought in the way their ancestors had done before they had crossed the Rhine or the North Sea: the armies were essentially tribal bands, made up of most of the able-bodied men in the community. The horse was little used in warfare; the only difference in the way of fighting between the richer and the poorer soldiers was the fact the richer men would have had slightly better weapons and perhaps better body armour.

This situation continued for over two centuries in continental Europe. The greatest battle of the eighth century, the battle of Tours, when the Frankish leader Charles Martel drove off the Moslems of Spain in AD 732, was won by an army that was entirely an infantry force. Very little was needed in the way of tactics, merely determination and energy. The army consisted of Charles's own personal bodyguard, and the levies called out from the areas of Frankland within reach. Little use was made of fortified positions and towns, at least not by the standards of the later Middle Ages, and the art of war in the eighth century consisted of gathering enough men to enter your enemy's lands, ravaging them to your heart's content, and either beating the enemy in the field if he decided to fight against you, or leaving the area, weighed down with plunder.

This method of warfare began to change quite drastically as the eighth century drew to its close. The great emperor Charlemagne became king of the Franks in AD 768, and embarked on a series of campaigns of conquest which would, at the end of his reign, see him ruling an empire from the Elbe to the Ebro, and the Straits of Dover to the River Tiber. Not having any brothers or male relatives, who would have divided the realm between them and caused a riot of civil war, Charles was able to direct all his attention to wars of conquest and conversion.

The sheer length of his campaigns, together with the necessity, as time went on, of fighting in distant lands, required him to possess an army which could be brought together reasonably quickly, and could march to the furthest ends of the lands under his domain. The old tribal levies were not adequate for this purpose, so he decided, over a period of years it seems, to depend on a smaller, better-equipped, mounted army, which would be able to travel fast and stay longer in the field. The result was that the armies he took with him on campaign gradually began to increase their quota of cavalry, until at the time of his death, in AD 814, almost the entire army of the Franks would consist of horsemen.

These changes, of course, meant a great deal of change in social organisation as well. The need for a permanent group of warriors, almost always on campaign, resulted in warfare becoming 'aristocratised'. The number of men serving in Charles's armies seems to have become lower as the horseman gradually became dominant on the battlefields of Europe. As warfare became an area in which the rich and titled were gradually taking control, the armies began to reduce in size, proportionate to the size of the population. By the beginning of the ninth century, it was estimated that it would take six men to equip one man to be sent to war. Taking into account the fact that the man in question would have to have a horse, mailshirt, lance, shield, helmet and sword, and have provisions to send him on his way, we can see how quickly the size of the armies decreased as time went on, and how the armoured and mounted knight would soon reign supreme on the battlefield. It is worth noting that the battle of Tours was won, in AD 732, by a Frankish force consisting entirely of infantry, while at the battle of Fontenoy, when Charlemagne's grandsons, Charles the Bald, Louis the German and Lothair the Emperor, fought each other with the Frankish empire as a prize, the armies of all the combatants were, it seems, mounted.

The chaos surrounding the collapse of the Carolingian empire was made even more acute by the coming of two of the most ferocious enemies the continent of Europe had ever seen: the Vikings and the Magyars. The former, coming on their longships from Norway and Sweden, ravaged the coasts of the empire from the Rhine to the Rhône. As these troops were only out for plunder, at least to begin with, they proved very elusive targets – once they had ravaged a district, they would move off to another, or return home. A force of quick-moving soldiers was required to catch them, or cut them off from their ships. The old tribal levies were far too slow for this purpose: a more localised and quick-moving force was required. This was seen as early as 866, when the king of the Franks, the treacherous, cowardly and incompetent Charles the Bald, seeing his realm ravaged by the sea-wolves, declared that any man who had a horse or was rich enough to afford one must come mounted to the mobilisation of the kingdom's host.

The demand for a mobile force to attack the kingdom's enemies began to gain force in the ninth century, and by the end of the Dark Ages the mounted knight would be dominant. This is shown by the fact that in the year 923, when Robert, king of the Franks, was killed at Soissons, he and his entire host were mounted and armed with lance, shield and dagger. It is to be noted that none of the mounted knights appeared to have a bow and arrow, unlike some of their ancestors under Charlemagne. This may suggest that the weight and complexity of their armour was increasing.

This change to the mounted knight would be seen across Christendom. In the lands to the east of the Rhine, where the great German dukedoms were ravaged by the raids of the Magyars, the horse archers from the plains of Hungary, there was the same insistence on making the armies of the kingdom mounted. The old tribal levies of the lands of the Saxons and Bavarians were even less capable of meeting these mounted archers than their cousins in the west were of meeting the Vikings. But the reforms of Henry the Fowler, the second German king, led to his subjects fighting on horse, rather than on foot. These reforms would bear fruition under the reign of Henry's son, the first German Emperor, Otto the Great, who managed to smash the Magyar menace once and for all at the battle of the Lechfeld in AD 955. At this battle, both sides consisted entirely of mounted men, and the winning side had far better armour than that of the losers.

The dominance of the mounted knight was accompanied by another reform, which could also be put at the door of Charlemagne: the growth of fortified towns and cities. The collapse of the Roman Empire meant also a collapse of the skills needed to keep in repair the walls of the great cities raised by the people on the Tiber. One is struck by the fact that the chronicles of the Dark Age tribes in England and Europe from AD 500 to AD 800 contain battles galore but comparatively few sieges, by the standards of the high Middle Ages. This decline of town and city life would be changed by Charles, a man of great energy and breadth of mind, and also of great determination and ruthlessness.

One of the weaknesses of the armies before the accession of Charles was their inability to hold the land they had conquered. Charles set about changing this by ensuring that whenever he occupied an enemy's land his hold would be guaranteed by building castles (called burghs). The Frankish armies adopted this comparatively simple idea very quickly. The conquests of Charles, from Saxony to Lombardy, from the Ebro to the Danube, were accompanied by the erection of fortifications of progressively more elaborate design. These ideas were not only useful in an army which was on the attack, but were even more necessary for a kingdom on the defence. The raids of the Vikings and Magyars made it essential for a region to have a place to which they could retire whenever they were attacked. In the east, Henry the Fowler ordered a huge number of towns to be surrounded by palisades or earthen walls, making it impossible for the Magyars to overrun them. In the west the Viking raids also proved a catalyst for the building of fortifications. On the orders of Charles the Bald, construction of fortified cities and bridges began on the river mouths where the Vikings were prone to attack.

These initiatives were to pay dividends in 885, when the Vikings besieged Paris. The city was able to repulse the attacks of the northmen, largely because it had been given a new set of fortifications on the orders of Charles the Bald. It is worth noting also that the army that eventually came to the relief of the city, led by an even more incompetent Carolingian, Charles the Fat, was entirely a mounted force, and could perhaps have smashed the Vikings if Charles, in a decision which was to cost him his crown, had not decided to bribe the Vikings to leave.

In the siege of Paris, we see the form of warfare that was to last in Europe for almost six centuries. A force, usually consisting of mounted troops, would ravage the lands of its enemies. The people under attack would take shelter within the walls of the nearest city, until a larger relieving army would come to drive off the attackers, leaving the country ravaged, but the towns in the hands of the defenders.

It is worth noting that most of the battles fought in the ensuing period would be battles fought to raise a siege, or repulse the relievers. The battle of Bannockburn was fought, according to some, to stop the fall of Stirling Castle in 1314; in 1204 King John was beaten outside the walls of Chateau-Gaillard trying to raise the siege; in 1141 King Stephen was beaten outside the walls of Lincoln trying to beat off a relieving army; in 1198 Richard I beat Philip Augustus outside Gisors, which Philip was attempting to besiege.

It is also interesting that the only kingdom in Europe which had, by the standards of the time, very few castles – England – saw, in 1066, three battles fought within a month of each other. Not one of these battles was really fought to take or relieve a city, and the fact that the Normans were able to conquer England so quickly, as more than one chronicler of the time noted, was because of the lack of walled cities. Scotland, where the walled city as we know it was almost non-existent, saw more than its fair share of kings killed in battle, and Malcolm IV was killed in the north-east of England, an area where there were very few fortifications indeed.

In effect, warfare became a matter of resources. The kingdom with the most resources could send in more and more men and material to ravage the land until their enemies gave in through sheer exhaustion, or until they were able to take by starvation or siege the castles of their opponents. This is the way Philip Augustus was able to take Normandy – not only did he have the inestimable advantage of fighting John, an exceptionally incompetent monarch, but the resources of the Capetian kingdom were greater (or, at any event, used far more wisely) than those of his Plantagenet opponent.

These changes in warfare would be seen to a remarkable degree in the campaign of 1138, when the new feudal host of Scotland would be seen in all its glory in the famous battle of the Standard.

6

The Battle of the Standard

When David invaded England in AD 1138, he gave as his reason that he was there to help his niece, Matilda the Empress, claim her throne. Cynics might claim that he was taking advantage of the opportunity of attacking while Stephen was down in the south, fighting rebels. David had a free hand to take some the north for himself.

The army that David took to the south in 1138 showed just how much he had managed to unite the Scots during his reign; he managed to mobilise practically all of the Scottish earldoms for his invasion. With him were not only the Norman knights who he had brought in with him in 1100, but the men of Galloway and the Highlands, men of the Lothian and Strathclyde, and, according to rather dubious sources, some mercenaries from Norway thrown in for good measure. The army must have numbered at least 10,000 men, which made it the largest Scottish army ever to invade England until the Civil War in the seventeenth century.

The fact that David managed to unite the clans and newcomers under his standard did not mean to say he could discipline them. When the Scottish army swept across the lands of Northumberland and Durham, even taking into account the exaggeration that was customary among the chroniclers of the time, they appear to have behaved with savage cruelty. The lands were ravaged, and according to some the Scots indulged in such atrocities as 'killing the monk at the altar and babes at the breast.' In August, this disparate horde reached Northallerton, in North Yorkshire, where they met their nemesis.

King Stephen, his hands full with the revolts in the south, sent two of his leading barons, Bernard de Balliol and Walter of Albemarle, along with their households, to help the Sheriff of Yorkshire, Walter L'Espec, who had ordered out the levies of Yorkshire to meet the Scots. To give them confidence, the ageing Archbishop of York, Thurstan, arranged for the banners of the three most important saints of Yorkshire, St Peter of Ripon, St John of Beverley, and St Wilfred of Ripon, to be put in a cart and taken with the army. They also took the banner of the godfather of northern saints, Cuthbert of Durham. The English army marched to Northallerton, and there took up their position a little to the north of the present-day town.

The organisation of both armies is very interesting. The English army was led by the descendants of the northern knights who had come across after 1066, leading the English levies of the north. The Scottish army was led by David, half Scottish and half Saxon, who had a Norman wife and whose leaders were also descendants of the Normans. The foot soldiers of the Lothian were the descendants of Anglo-Saxons who had left England in disgust after 1066. The rest of the Scottish force consisted of the 'true Scots', who were suspicious of both the English and the Normans. This very interesting ethnic mix would have catastrophic repercussions for David in the ensuing conflict.

The English army took up their position at Northallerton on 22 August 1138. They were about 10,000 strong. We are told that they were organised on foot in one deep line, with archers, of whom there were a great number, interspersed among the knights and foot soldiers. Behind the line was a small baggage guard.

When David saw the positioning of the English army, he ordered his mounted knights to dismount and lead the Scottish army in the assault on the English line. The men of the Highlands and Galloway would follow them, and the archers would follow in the flanks of the force. This idea was greeted with anger by many of the Highlanders, who resented the fact that the Normans were given preferential treatment on the battlefield as well as in the council chamber. Led by the Earl of Strathearn, they refused to give precedence to the Norman and English strangers. A furious altercation broke out, which was only halted when David ordered his knights to mount their horses, and the men of Galloway to take the vanguard. The result was that the Scottish centre consisted of the Highlanders and the men of Galloway, and the Norman horse were put under the command of David's son, Prince Henry, on the right wing. Meanwhile, the men of the Lothian, together with a small bodyguard for King David, were in reserve.

Before the battle started, Bernard de Balliol, who, like most of the Norman knights, held land in both England and Scotland, rode to David to consent to peace terms. He pointed out a very interesting fact: as David was more Norman than Scottish and he was more Norman than English, why were they fighting each other? But this logical argument was drowned out by the catcalls of the younger knights, who denounced Balliol as a traitor.

Balliol promptly renounced his homage to David, and rode off to join the English army.

With the formalities over, the men of Galloway and the Highlands opened the battle with shouts of 'Albany, Albany' and rushed forward to attack. When they came within range of the English archers, they were met with a hail of arrows, which felled them by the hundred, 'many of them looking like a hedgehogs with the shafts still sticking their bodies' according to one chronicler, implying that these Scottish savages had got exactly what they deserved.

The Gallowegians and the Highlanders recoiled from the arrows; their chiefs were nearly all slain, since, following the tradition of the time, they led from the front. Their followers halted, turned tail and fled, almost overrunning the divisions of King David. While this was going on, Prince Henry led his division in a charge on the English line and, after savage fighting, hewed his way through and managed to get to the baggage guard of the English. In doing so, however, his knights were slaughtered. With only nineteen men left, Henry saw that he would get no support, so he ordered his men to cast off their badges and ride round the English army to rejoin their comrades.

Seeing the Gallowegians and Highlanders retreat, the men of the Lothian decided that discretion was the better part of valour and promptly decamped from the battlefield. Meanwhile, David, seeing his army collapse before his eyes, ordered the retreat. So ended the battle of Northallerton, the greatest Scottish-English conflict since Brunanburgh, and not to be surpassed until Stirling Bridge. At least 2,000 Scots were slain in the battle, which forced David to turn to negotiation in order to claim the lands of Northumbria.

Although he launched a few raids into England during Stephen's civil wars, in general David's reign was a peaceful one. The new aristocracy, apart from the rather unpleasant glitch at Northallerton, settled well into the lands of the Scots. But the last years of David's life were sad: both his wife, Matilda, and his son, Henry, died before him. Although he managed to settle the succession to everybody's satisfaction (Henry's sons by his wife, Ada of Northumberland, being designated heirs to the throne), David never seemed to get over the deaths of his wife and son. He himself died in 1153. He had taken over control of a wild and turbulent kingdom and improved the administration, learning and economy of the land, doing so with remarkably little bloodshed or force. As England can claim that its greatest monarch was Alfred the Great, Scotland can surely state, even with the Bruce casting his giant shadow, that David was the greatest of all the Scottish monarchs.

7

The Maiden and the Lyon

One of the most important changes of David's reign was the general acceptance of the law of primogeniture, in which land descends from father to eldest son, or to the nearest male heir of the eldest son. The old Pictish custom of choosing the king from the most able of the sons of the royal family was now ignored, and David's grandsons were the next tenants of the throne.

Malcolm IV was the eldest of the three sons of Henry, David's only son. Although he was given the name of his great-grandfather, he appears to have had little of the ferocity, energy, brutality or even intelligence of his ancestor. He seems to have been a vain, weak and petulant character, and was nicknamed, with customary Scottish bluntness, 'the maiden'. The nickname apparently came not only from his failure to marry, but from the fact that he was a somewhat effeminate and uninspired individual.

David had taken the opportunity of having his grandson sent on a sort of grand tour around Scotland along with the most important of the Scottish earls, the Earl of Fife, whose duty it was to take the heir to the coronation stone at Scone, where he would be officially declared king of the Scots. But Malcolm was no hero-king: the greatest incident of his reign was when one Somerled, a great lord of the Highlands, managed to expel the last of the Viking lords from the Western Isles. Malcolm neither helped nor hindered this action, being preoccupied by the behaviour of his rather tempestuous southern brother, Henry II of England, the first of the buccaneering Plantaganet dynasty.

A tough and devious individual who combined total duplicity with a surprising degree of fairness and a staggering degree of learning, Henry managed to keep Malcolm on a short leash by the simple expedient of threatening to hold back the revenues of the Honour of Huntington if Malcolm did not do Henry's bidding. As these revenues were vital to the Scottish economy, Malcolm, to the fury of some of his more insular subjects, duly came south to do homage to Henry, give up any claims to the lands of Cumbria and Northumbria, and accompany Henry on one of his unending wars in France. To show his gratitude, Henry knighted Malcolm (a move which offended many Scots, who thought this could have been done by a Scotsman) and allowed him to keep the revenues of Huntington.

Malcolm died in 1165 and was succeeded by William, surnamed the Lyon. William's heroic nickname came from his adoption of the royal emblem, the lion rampant, as the Scottish royal banner, rather than the sign of the boar, which had sufficed for his Pictish ancestors – another sign of how the feudal system was now exerting its pressure.

William managed to strengthen the governmental system by the mere fact that he reigned so long: forty-nine years, which was a record for the times. His longevity as a ruler appears to have been due less to the fact that he was a dynamic and far-seeing monarch, which he most certainly was not, than to the fact that Henry II, who was still Scotland's southern brother, was a fairly equable individual by the standard of the times, as illustrated by the following incident.

In July 1174, Henry was reeling from an attack by his sons in the great lands he held in France. He was the whipping-boy of Christendom in general, as a result of some of his more brainless knights having killed Thomas Becket, the Archbishop of Canterbury. William, realising that the best time to kick a man was when he was down, launched an invasion of England to regain the lands of

Northumbria. Unfortunately, when besieging the castle of Alnwick, near the place where William's great-grandfather Malcolm III had met his end, nobody seems to have taken the elementary precaution of sending out scouts. A much smaller English army, under the cover of a convenient fog, approached the besieged town to find the Scottish camp in no sort of order whatsoever. On seeing this force, William, apparently without bothering to regroup his forces, promptly galloped against the English, crying heroically 'Now we shall see who is a knight!' At this point, an unnamed individual killed his horse with a lance.

William was captured, his army scattered, and the Lyon was taken as a prize to London. Just to teach him a lesson, his feet were tied beneath his horse, and he was incarcerated in the Tower of London, where a number of Scotsmen would spend enforced periods of leisure over the next few centuries. But Henry, unlike most of his contemporaries, proved to be a magnanimous victor. He did not demand any land, although he put garrisons in some of the main Scottish cities and forced William to become his vassal, not just for Huntingdon but for the whole of Scotland. Tough as these terms appear to be, Scotland lost no land, was not ravaged by foreign armies and, of course, kept the ever-important revenues of Huntingdon.

When William was released, he found himself saddled with a wife whom Henry had forced him to take, Ermingarde de Beaumont. He was also forced to attend the English king whenever it took Henry's fancy. Henry, however, was by this time a mellower man than in his turbulent youth, and the relationship between the two seemed to become quite pleasant. William's main concerns were dealing with revolts in the perennially unstable Galloway and Ross areas, and founding some abbeys.

The knotty problem of Scotland's independence was seemingly solved by the behaviour of Richard I. In 1189, fresh from helping his father, Henry II, into an early grave, Richard was eager to give greater scope to his talents for slaughter by embarking on the Third Crusade. As the subjects of the English king realised, this meant money:

crusades required a lot of sacrifice for very little benefit. Richard solved some of his cash problems by selling off his rights as overlord to William, for 10,000 marks. This so-called 'Quitclaim of Canterbury' also guaranteed the independence of the Scottish Church from the rule of the Archbishops of Canterbury. From this date, the Church would become one of the most patriotic members of the Scottish establishment, with rather interesting repercussions a few years later.

Richard's death outside the walls of Challus, in an obscure petty siege, brought to the throne the most deranged and murderous of the Plantagenet dynasty, John. Throughout his career, John would manage to bring the Plantagenet realm to its knees and, by accepting the principles of the Magna Carta, would give constitutional lawyers something to argue about for centuries.

William the Lyon, taking advantage of John's eternal wars in France, began raiding the marches of Northumbria. John, acting for once with decision and wisdom, marched north, faced William down, and forced his foolish northern brother to hand over money and hostages to guarantee his good behaviour. William died in 1214, having managed by the sheer length of time he was on the throne to ensure continuity and stability to Scotland, and to make it richer and more peaceful.

He was succeeded by his son, Alexander II, who would prove to be a more mature and perceptive character than his father. Taking advantage of John's troubles with his nobles, who were rather distressed at having a monarch who was in the habit of killing his relatives with his own hand (he had murdered his nephew Arthur in 1205, and dumped his body in the Seine), Alexander began raiding the borders between the two kingdoms. But once John had lost the main part of the Plantagenet lands in France, and had been excommunicated by the Pope, he found himself in England with a little more time on his hands. He therefore decided to 'chase the fox cub from its lair' and, using wealth he had acquired by confiscating the monies the English Church was sending to the Pope in Rome, he gathered an army to teach his northern neighbour a lesson.

For several months, John and Alexander waged war in the Borders. Unlike most of John's campaigns, this little escapade was on the whole successful. Berwick and Dunbar went up in flames; castles were erected. By 1217, Alexander was forced to make peace with his southern neighbour, and was guaranteed the Honour of Huntington, and some small lands on the border. This ending of the war between the two kingdoms was the harbinger of a long peace. It gave Alexander a chance to settle some of the troubles afflicting his kingdom, such as the perennially unstable west and north. He pacified the north, and at least managed to keep Galloway quiet. In 1221, in York, he married Joanne, the sister of John's son, Henry III.

Although Alexander's reign was peaceful, he was plagued by a problem that was the curse of Christendom at this time: the succession. By 1238, he and Joanne had not had any children, a terrible state of affairs when so much depended on a peaceful succession at the top of the feudal ladder. Alexander's heir presumptive at the start of the reign had been his uncle David, the youngest brother of the Lyon and the Maiden, who held the earldom of Huntingdon. David and his son, John the Scot, had both died, and John (like a surprising number of medieval nobles) had been childless. This left the lucrative Honour of Huntingdon, together with the Scottish succession, in abeyance. The heirs to the Honour of Huntingdon were, ominously, three women, which meant that if one of them succeeded to the throne of Scotland, her husband would be – by virtue of the wife – king of the Scots. This was not the sort of succession which went down well with anyone in the Middle Ages, as a man who was king through his wife did not get the same respect as a man born to the role.

To make things even more worrying, the two eldest girls, Margaret and Isabel, were married to two of the most powerful men in Scotland: Alan, lord of the ever-turbulent Galloway, and Robert Bruce of Annandale, whose descendants would lead such interesting lives. If Alexander died without heirs, it would mean an immediate dispute as to which of the husbands would rule in the name of his wife. Alexander realised the problems facing the kingdom and, taking into account the volatile nature of Galloway, decided in 1238 to make Robert Bruce, the husband of Isabel of Huntingdon, the heir presumptive to the throne. This action, however, would not produce consequences for another half-century; Joanne of England died in 1238, and Alexander married in haste one of the European noblewomen then available on the marriage market. This was Marie de Coucy, daughter of one of the greatest barons of the French kingdom, whose castle (until it was blown up by the German general Ludendorff in 1918) dominated the area to the north of Paris for centuries. Marie gave Alexander a healthy son in 1240.

The only person who appeared to be upset with this state of affairs was Henry of England, who, with typical petulance, believed that he should have decided who was to be the next wife of the king of the Scots. He showed his displeasure in typically spiteful fashion: he made sure the revenues from the earldom of Huntingdon were not paid to Alexander, but to the three daughters of John the Scot, and he declared that in future no Scot could hold an English earldom. Enraged by his former brother-in-law's behaviour, Alexander began to mobilise his troops on the frontier; Henry, deciding to take part in the sport of kings, marched an army to the north. But wiser counsel prevailed, and the two kings made peace at Newcastle. The terms are now a little obscure, but one of the items was that the new heir to the Scots, also called Alexander, would marry one of Henry's daughters.

Apart from a further stand-off in 1244, the two kingdoms were as peaceful as any neighbours could be in the Middle Ages. The fact that the earldom of Huntingdon was now divided and had gone to the daughters of John the Scot did not seem to affect the amicable relations between the kingdoms, which were displayed by the great event of 1251: the marriage of Alexander III and Margaret of England, the daughter of Henry III. The reason for Alexander's early marriage was that his father, Alexander II, had decided to mount an expedition to the north, to solve the problem of his ever-rebellious Celtic subjects, and wished to secure his southern frontiers.

The expedition did not have the desired result, however, as Alexander died of a fever in 1249, on the Isle of Kerrara.

Alexander III was only nine years old when he succeeded to the throne, which caused an immediate squabble between the ruling families of the day as to who would rule in the king's name. A lot of ink has been wasted on whether the dispute over this affair was the precursor of the wars that were to explode in the kingdom after the death of Alexander III. This seems unlikely: after all, whenever there was a royal minority in any kingdom, there was an immediate scuffle to see who would be the *de facto* ruler. The reign of Edward V in England and the numerous Stewart minorities of later days would illustrate this.

The two main rivals for the control of the throne were the Comyns of Buchan, one of the families introduced by the multi-talented David I, and Alan Durward, Earl of Atholl, one of the few truly Celtic lords of the land. Though the quarrels were sometimes divisive, there appears to have been no outbreak of open warfare between the rival factions, something that the English in the minority of Henry III could not claim to have achieved, nor the French court in the minority of Louis XI. This shows just how settled most of the kingdom now was, and also shows that the works of David, Alexander II, and even William the Lyon, had borne considerable fruit.

When Alexander III reached maturity, he took the affairs of the kingdom into his own hands. He proved to be a worthy monarch, the last of the house of Canmore. Even if we take into account what happened in the next few years, when the level of slaughter made many people reminisce for the good old days, Alexander appears to have kept a stable peace over the land and maintained good relations with his southern neighbour. He met Henry III in York in 1251, when he married his daughter, Margaret of England, and accepted knighthood at his hands. The festivities, personally organised by Henry, who was adept at putting on a show, were regarded as sensational. According to the chronicler Matthew Paris, Henry was attended by 1,000 knights (Alexander was attended by a mere sixty).

After the customary medieval brawls as to who was to be lodged where, the festivities went on full blast for several days, and an astonishing quantity of food was consumed: seventy boars, 1,300 hares, 290 pheasants and 68,500 loaves of bread, which goes to show that over-indulgence in food is not a twenty-first-century luxury.

The culmination of these festivities – the knighthood and the wedding – was somewhat diluted when Henry, after he had knighted Alexander, invited the ten-year-old to pay homage to him for the kingdom of Scotland. Alexander's advisers had warned him that Henry would take this tack, and he answered by saying 'He had come to York to be married, not answer so difficult a matter.' Henry seemed to accept this precocious reply, and the wedding to Margaret went off without a hitch on 26 December 1251. Observers of the festivities would have found it very hard to believe that just over sixty years later, the heir to the father of the bride would die campaigning in the kingdom of his new brother-in-law, and that the father's grandson would suffer the most catastrophic English defeat between the battle of Hastings and the fall of Singapore – and would, as a direct result of the wars in Scotland, suffer a brutal and sadistic death at Berkeley Castle. Alexander, his new Plantaganet wife, and his entourage, left York apparently quite contented with the way things had turned out. Margaret proved capable of fulfilling the main role expected of a medieval wife, and began to produce heirs at a rate which, if not equal to the rate at which the Spanish infanta Eleanor of Castile produced children for Edward I, was at least prolific enough to ensure the succession. Margaret was born in 1260, followed by Alexander and David.

Conditions were so peaceful in Scotland after Alexander took over the reins of power that some of his nobles thought they had the leisure to take part in the Barons' War in England, precipitated by Henry's idea of making one of his sons, Edmund, king of Sicily. At the battle of Lewes, the Barons, led by Simon de Montfort, captured some of these Scottish nobles after Henry, inevitably, was defeated. The fact that some of his leading nobles were now in English dungeons apparently did not have any effect on Alexander, who was now ruling with the firmness and moderation which was expected of a medieval king, and which was conspicuously lacking in his southern brother. The battle of Evesham in 1265 put paid to the ambitions of de Montfort, and left the Lord Edward as his father's main prop in his later years. Edward went on a crusade – a sure sign in medieval times that a kingdom was at peace. He was in Sicily, on his way home, when he heard the news of his father's death. In November 1272, the Lord Edward became Edward I, king of England. Because of his great size and length of leg (he stood 6ft 3in tall and was the tallest man to be king of the English up to this time), he was known as Edward Longshanks, and was to be remembered by future generations as the Hammer of the Scots.

8

The Final Years of Peace: 1275–1289

Edward's return to England in 1274 meant that he and Alexander could renew their friendship. Alexander attended Edward's coronation in August 1275, and the knotty problem of homage to England was settled to everyone's satisfaction. The relations between the two kings appear to have been excellent. The only cloud on the horizon as far as Alexander was concerned was the death of his wife in 1275, and the deaths of his two sons in 1281 and 1284. The letters that the two monarchs sent to one other regarding these bereavements went far beyond the normal protocol and civilities of the time. The death of his sons meant that if Alexander could not produce more heirs, the next in line to the Scottish throne would be his granddaughter, the child of his daughter Margaret, who had married the king of Norway in 1281. She produced a daughter who was also called Margaret, the famous 'Maid of Norway', and died in childbirth in 1283.

Now that Alexander's sons were dead, it became imperative both for the Maid of Norway to be officially named as heiress to the throne of the Scots, and for Alexander to get married again. After the death of his eldest son, the Lord Alexander, in 1284, Alexander immediately ordered his magnates to swear homage to his granddaughter, which they did with alacrity. Alexander then had to decide which was the most eligible princess available on the medieval marriage market, and his choice fell on one of the daughters of the Count of Dreux – a direct descendant of Louis VI (known as the Fat), the king of France in the twelfth century.

The wedding went ahead in Jedburgh in October 1285, with the usual festivities and minus the brawls, murders and thievery which were generally associated with royal weddings at the time. The only glitches in the programme were an apparition that appeared at the end of a procession during the wedding feast, and then promptly disappeared, and an accusation by the chronicler of Lanercost, a monastery near Carlisle, that the new queen was not the sort of woman who could be trusted, and that indeed she had taken vows to be a nun.

Yolande had unfortunately not fallen pregnant by the night of 18 March 1286, when, instead of finding a warm bed in Kinghorn, the king of the Scots found a cantankerous horse which threw him to his death off the cliffs of Fife. He therefore died without a direct male heir. There was a well-known phrase in the Middle Ages: 'Woe to thee, oh kingdom whose ruler is a fool or a child!' This saying would prove to be calamitously true.

9

The Struggle for the Throne: Bruce *v.* Balliol

T he death of King Alexander caused consternation among the Scots. This can be seen by his precipitate burial in Dunfermline Abbey on 29 March 1286, and also by the fact that a parliament was called to meet at Scone on 2 April. The proceedings of this parliament showed just how much toughness and flexibility there was about a medieval kingdom, and proved that, to begin with at least, all the leading personages of Scotland appeared anxious to find a solution to the problem of the succession.

With commendable alacrity, a form of government was agreed upon. This was the famous 'six guardians'. This group consisted of two earls, Alexander Comyn, Earl of Buchan, and Duncan, Earl of Fife; two churchmen, William Fraser, bishop of St Andrew's, and Robert Wishart, bishop of Glasgow; James Stewart, the lord Steward; and John Comyn, Lord of Badenoch. This combination appears to mirror the country's power structure at the time: the Comyn clan, due to a mixture of skill and strategic marriages, were the most important clan in Scotland.

The settlement, although seemingly reasonable, was not to the taste of the Bruces of Annandale. Over the past few years, this family had risen through the feudal ranks to become one of the great families of Scotland. The head of the family was Robert Bruce, Lord of Annandale, known as Robert the Competitor, and formerly heir-presumptive to the throne. The family's fortunes had taken a sudden turn for the better in 1273 when Robert the Competitor's son, also called Robert, married Marjory, sole heiress to the great earldom of Carrick. This marriage was undoubtedly a love match, and Marjory accomplished her main duty as a medieval woman by giving birth to a son on 11 July. This would be the famous Robert the Bruce.

By his marriage to Marjory, Robert (now known for reasons of clarity as Robert II) became, in his wife's name, the Earl of Carrick, and one of the great lords of the land. The fact that none of them were given a seat on the Council of the Guardians was seen by the clan as a deliberate insult. Early in 1286, the Bruces and their allies seized the royal castles of Wigtown and Dumfries in the south-west, which acted as a link to the Bruce lands in Annandale and to the lands of Carrick. It is not known whether this was merely a grab for territory – the acquisition of which was one of the main roles of any nobleman – or a ploy to strengthen their family against the Comyns. But the news that came from the islands in the north would irredeemably shatter the peace of the kingdom.

10

The Maid of Norway

Upon the news of Alexander's death, messengers were sent to Edward I. Edward made no attempt to interfere in the running of the kingdom of the north; he was in Gascony, administering his lands in France, when he was told of the appointment of the Guardians as rulers of Scotland. The next three years were very peaceful for the Scots, which suggests that despite the power-grab of the Bruces, there was a genuine feeling that violence was to be avoided at all costs. These years were notable only for the death of one of the Guardians, Alexander of Buchan, from natural causes, and for the death of the other earl, Duncan of Fife, by decidedly unnatural means. Described as being 'treacherous and greedy beyond the normal bounds of men', Duncan was murdered by his own household, and was buried unmourned and unlamented in 1289. No other Guardians were appointed, leaving the gang of four in control of the destiny of Scotland.

The necessity of the Maid coming to Scotland to claim her birthright was of course the main preoccupation of the country's rulers at this time. Reflecting the close relationship between the kingdoms, a meeting between Scottish, Norwegian and English representatives was arranged at Salisbury in 1289, to arrange for the journey of the Maid from Norway and (of equal importance) to settle the matter of her marriage. It was agreed that she should come to Scotland and, most likely, that she should marry Edward's son, also called Edward.

Some later historians of the nationalist school think that this was a capitulation to Edward by the Scottish representatives. However, the two kingdoms had been at peace now for almost fifty years, a very long time by the brutal standards of the age. It was almost a habit for Scottish kings to marry English princesses, and the Scottish representatives were very careful to guarantee the independence of the Scottish kingdom in the ensuing talks. This is shown by the fact that at Brigham, in 1290, the leading representatives of Scotland accepted the conditions of the treaty of Salisbury. They seemed to ignore the fact that a line had been inserted into the treaty which said 'saving the right of our said lord (the future king) and any whomsoever, which has pertained to him, before the time of the present agreement'. It is unclear whether Edward was taking the chance to make Scotland a vassal state.

To begin with, Edward (ever the opportunist) occupied the Isle of Man, an island only recently taken under Scottish suzerainty. He also appointed one of the most pugnacious of his vassals, Anthony Beck, as high lieutenant in Scotland, despite the fact that neither the Maid nor Edward was present in the kingdom. We begin to see here Edward's growing ambitions concerning the affairs of Scotland.

The great men of Scotland assembled at Perth in September, to greet the Maid who was now their lady and queen. For some reason, the king of Norway, Eric, delayed sending the Maid to Scotland. She was sent to her kingdom only in September 1290, a notoriously stormy time of the year, and was soon driven by storms to the Isles of Orkney. There, to the utter consternation of the Scots, she died in the arms of the bishop of Bergen, some say of pure seasickness. The last of the line of Canmore was dead, and the Scots now faced a hideous future.

II

King Bruce? King Balliol?

The news of the Maid's death shattered the bonds which had held the Scottish kingdom together for so long. Who was to be the new ruler? To find out who the candidates were, it is necessary to go back to the days of King David. David's youngest grandson, also called David, had three daughters, of whom the two eldest each married Scottish nobles. The direct descendant of the eldest daughter was John Balliol. The second daughter, Isabel, had married Robert Bruce of Annandale, whose son Robert was still alive, and had been pronounced heir-presumptive by Alexander when he was still without heirs himself.

Who would be the ruler of Scotland, Bruce or Balliol? This would be the cause of appalling suffering in both England and Scotland for decades. Very soon after the news of the Maid's death, Robert Bruce (I) marched on Perth with a great following, while Balliol proclaimed himself heir of Scotland. The problem was compounded by the fact that Balliol's sister Eleanor had married the heir to the vast Comyn earldom of Buchan. In effect, one of the claimants to the Scottish throne had now allied himself to the most powerful clan in Scotland, leaving the Bruces even more marginalised in the affairs of the Scottish kingdom. A more volatile arrangement could not have been imagined.

At this point, Edward of England, who had been asked by several Scottish nobles for his opinion regarding who was to be the new king, marched north to decide the Scottish problem for himself. It should be pointed out that, although Edward's behaviour up to now had been opportunistic, he had not really given the Scots any cause for complaint. However, an incident that occurred while he was travelling north was to completely change his behaviour and have catastrophic consequences for all concerned. It was responsible for decades of slaughter on both sides of the border. His wife, the English queen, Eleanor of Castile, died of a fever in Lincolnshire.

The news of her death came as a shattering blow to Edward; he had married her in Castile in 1254 and, unlike most medieval marriages, the relationship turned into a genuine love match. In marked contrast to the more sedentary habits of the other queens of the time, Eleanor had accompanied Edward on his campaigns and travels throughout Christendom. She had acted as a restraining influence on him while she lived. From now on, embittered over his loss and perhaps realising how dangerous everyday life could be, even for a man brought up in the highest ranks of medieval nobility, Edward became a changed man. The savage Plantaganet temper became even more pronounced; his twisting of the law regarding Scottish affairs, perhaps a sign that he wanted to unify the British Isles before he died, became ever more apparent. The Scots would suffer for the death of the Spanish Infanta to a degree they could never have imagined.

The details regarding Queen Eleanor's funeral kept Edward busy for several months, and it was not until the spring of 1291 that he had the time to come north and deal with the Scottish matter. Although it was quite clear that the two main contenders for the throne would be Bruce and Balliol, a pack of other hopefuls, in true medieval fashion, put in claims for the right to be king. These individuals and their representatives, now known popularly as 'The Competitors', gathered at Norham, on the Tweed, to await Edward's arrival.

When he came to meet them, the Scottish were in for a very rude shock, since Edward demanded that he be acknowledged overlord of Scotland before he adjudicated on who would be king. The Scottish appear to have been shocked by this demand and, given the circumstances, had every reason to be. Edward gave them a day to come up with a reply, and then a further three weeks. During this time, with the ruthless duplicity that was becoming ever more apparent in his character, he ordered the levies of the north of England up to the Tweed, in order to show the Scots the iron fist in his not-very-velvet glove.

The bishop of Glasgow, Robert of Wishart, who would play a very ambiguous role in the coming tragedy, composed a reply stating in effect that no one had any knowledge of Edward's right to be overlord of Scotland. Edward, however, stated categorically that no adjudication would be forthcoming unless his claim was met. This put the Scottish in a quandary. In the first place, Edward was not the sort of man to be gainsaid. Furthermore, a great many Scottish nobles held land in England, and if they disagreed with Edward it would be only too easy for him to confiscate their lands.

After much quarrelling, the Scots eventually gave in to Edward's demands. Edward went on what can only described as a grand tour of Scotland, putting his own troops in the royal castles of Scotland and demanding homage from the great men of the realms before he was willing to give his views on who was to occupy the throne. Despite the ruthlessness he had shown to the Scots in demanding his rights as overlord, it cannot be argued that he fudged the question of who was to be king. In Berwick, in August 1291, a court of claims was set up. Compared to the speed Edward had shown in demanding homage, the sessions of the court dragged on interminably – although this is not altogether surprising, since a grand total of thirteen persons made claims for the kingship.

Edward was scrupulous about deciding who had the main claim, and not even his worst enemies could fault his behaviour here. Every candidate had his claim scrupulously investigated and, by the laws of primogeniture, it soon became apparent that the three claimants to the throne with the greatest legal right were the descendants of David, Earl of Huntingdon. As John Balliol was the descendant of the eldest of David's three daughters, Balliol was undoubtedly next

in line for the succession according to the laws then extant in western Christendom. On 17 November 1292, Edward gave his decision:
Balliol would be the new king of the Scots.

If anyone had believed that Edward would be satisfied with deciding who would be the next king, they would be sadly mistaken. At
the official enthronement of Balliol at Scone on 30 November, the
Earl of Fife, who traditionally had the right to lead the new king to
the coronation stone, was unable to carry out his task, as he was an
infant. To show who was boss, Edward ordered one of his own men,
an Englishman, John de St John, to take over this role.

Immediately after his coronation, John Balliol went back to
England to do formal homage to Edward for his kingdom. With this
unpleasant but necessary task undertaken, Balliol returned to his new
realm. He has been depicted by historians as a feeble and ineffectual
man, entirely dependent on one faction of the lords of the land (the
Comyns). It is true that from the few royal acts extant in this period, the picture emerges of a man who, if not overwhelmed by his
responsibilities, certainly did not take a firm grip on affairs. This was
left to his relatives, the Comyns, who had of course been running
the government for years. But this was not necessarily a bad thing,
and some important administrative changes took place in Balliol's
reign, such as the creation of new sheriffdoms in the Western Isles, to
extend the power of the throne.

Balliol could, it seems, have been an effectual but not very inspir-
ing monarch, content to slog away at the council table – the sort of
man, of course, who would not appeal to bloodthirsty historians of
later days. That he did not become this monarch is almost wholly
due to Edward of England, whose behaviour after the crowning of
Balliol has shocked even some of his most enthusiastic apologists. To
begin with, Edward made his hapless neighbour free him from any
promises that Edward had made to him regarding the freedom of the
Scottish crown. Then, in what can only be described as a series of
deliberately engineered incidents, Balliol was called down to London
repeatedly to hear appeals from his own subjects, made by Edward's

own lawyers, despite this being quite clearly contrary to the treaty of Bingham.

The protests of Balliol and his council fell on deaf ears, since Edward seemed determined to reduce Scotland to a mere sheriffdom of England. Balliol and some of his councillors duly went south on several occasions to hear Scottish appeals in English courts. Treated with studied discourtesy, Balliol and Scotland seemed to be destined to be ground to dust by Edward over the next few years. Even Edward, however, went too far with the next set of demands he made on the Scots: a set of claims that would lead directly to the Wars of Independence. Edward Longshanks ordered the Scottish to assist him in his wars against the French king, Phillip IV, a man even more duplicitous then Edward himself.

The demand that they fight in a war which did not concern them in the slightest enraged many of the Scots, though Balliol, by now an almost completely broken man, seemed willing to agree. Balliol was almost completely sidelined by his own councillors, who formed a new council of twelve nobles, while a treaty of alliance was signed with the French at Dunfermline Abbey in February 1296. Edward, on hearing of the alliance (for which he was entirely to blame), was enraged, and promptly ordered an invasion of Scotland, which had been only too willing to accept vassal status from him.

12

Berwick and Dunbar: An End and a Beginning

T he campaign of 1296, which ended in total capitulation by the Scots, has been described as the final example of the uselessness of the rule of Balliol. In less than six months, the Scots would see their most prosperous town brutally sacked, their king humiliated, and their nobles defeated in battle. A closer look, however, shows that this was not the case at all.

After sending a letter to Edward stating his formal renunciation of homage, and including the statement 'We cannot any longer endure these injures, insults and grievous wrongs nor these hostile attacks, nor can we remain in you fealty and homage (which, it may be said, were extorted by extreme coercion on your part) and we desire to assert ourselves against you...', Balliol was faced with the problem of how to resist his deadly opponent. It should be pointed out that the population of England at that time was roughly 3,000,000, and that of Scotland was about one sixth of that. In an age when the number of able-bodied men a nation could put into the field was a guarantor of its military strength, this discrepancy was a fearsome one.

Furthermore, the unity of the realm was nothing like as definite as when David paid his unwanted visit to Northallerton in 1138. The fact that Balliol was able to last so long on the throne of Scotland was due to his relationship with the Comyn clan. The Bruces, losers in the claim to the throne, were quite naturally opposed to Balliol and his supporters and, according to the rather dubious 'Scotichronicon', had been promised the throne by Edward if they helped him in his attack in Scotland. The position of the Bruces regarding Edward Longshanks had been ambiguous for years. The death in 1295 of the elder Bruce, Robert the Competitor, had left the affairs of the clan in the hands of his son, Robert Bruce II, Earl of Carrick who, it appears, was none too willing to accept it. His son, the famous Robert Bruce III, now comes rather more into the spotlight, casting an unforgettable shadow over the history of the Scots.

The Bruces could hardly oppose King Edward, to whom they had given fealty and from whom they held land (like nearly every other leading nobleman of the time). If they opposed Balliol, it could be argued that they were acting as traitors to the kingdom, a fact that nationalist historians appear to ignore when they denounce Balliol. In typically medieval fashion, the Bruce family decided to cast in its lot with the stronger power, and 1296 found the Bruces, father and son, holding the English fortress of Carlisle on the West March of the Anglo-Scottish frontier, of which they happened to be governors. When, in March 1296, the muster of the Scots was ordered by the Council to meet at Caddonlee near Edinburgh, a significant number of men did not turn up to fight the English. The Bruces were not there, nor was Patrick, Earl of Dunbar, and nor were quite a few of the commonalty, who were most likely bewildered at the antics of their betters.

Quite apart from the disparity in numbers between the English and the Scots, and the Scottish lack of cohesion when confronted by Edward Longshanks, the Scots had another problem which has been strangely ignored by the historians: they had very little experience of fighting. The preceding decades in Scotland had been, by the admittedly low standards of the time, extremely peaceful. The last time any of the Scots had fought in anger was when some of their number, who should have known better, had clashed with Henry III at the battle of Lewes, in 1264. Apart from the handful of men who had fought on the crusades, no other military experience was available to them. Balliol, in effect, was going to war, with a kingdom which was bitterly divided, against an enemy which would outnumber him – an enemy which, given Edward Longshanks's predilection for fighting his neighbours every day of the week, was very experienced at warfare.

The campaign started on its inevitable course in March 1296, when Edward ordered the mustering of the feudal host of England at Wark, near the Tweed. At least 18,000 men seem to have been mobilised, led by a man thirsting for revenge against what he considered the contumacious behaviour of his northern neighbours. The opening round of the war began when John Comyn, the son of the Earl of Buchan, led a raid into the Borders and swept up to the walls of Carlisle, then of course being held by the Bruces. This raid, which could hardly have lessened the rivalry of the two houses, was beaten off with ease by the Bruces. Comyn consequently ignored the huge fortress and rode on into Northumberland, leaving a trail of destruction behind him.

By launching an attack through the West March, Comyn was probably trying to make Edward turn and face him, as would happen on a number of occasions in later years. Edward, however, ignored this attack and marched his army to Berwick, the most populous city of Scotland at this date. The events that followed emphasised just how peaceful the land of the Scots had been over the past few years, and made it clear why Edward Longshanks was such a fearful enemy: the city was protected merely by a timber stockade, more of a customs wall than a means of defence. The citadel was held by William, Lord of Douglas, whose son would cast a rather different shadow on Anglo-Scottish relations several years later.

Edward brought up his navy from Newcastle, and surrounded the city by both land and sea. He ordered an attack from the sea which, owing to the currents or the incompetence of the captain, ran aground. The Scots gleefully swept out and burned the stricken vessel. Two other ships in the fleet somehow caught fire and were destroyed. Overjoyed by this feat, the Scottish on the walls of the city yelled insults at the besiegers, probably asking the English where their tails were. (For some reason, the English were popularly supposed to have to have devils' tails hanging between their legs).

Edward Longshanks hated to be opposed in anything, especially in battle. In response to the insults, he ordered his trumpeters to sound the advance. The army swept forward, scaled the palisade apparently with no trouble at all, and proceeded to utterly annihilate the Scots. For two days, the English army sacked the city, which before the attack had been among the richest and most populous in Scotland. 30 March 1296 marks the beginning of the hatred that would exist for so many centuries between the two nations. Only a group of Flemish merchants in their own 'Red Hall' appear to have put up any resistance. For two days the slaughter went on unchecked, while Edward Longshanks rode through the city to see for him the way war was waged in the thirteenth century. It was said that only the sight of a pregnant woman being killed, and her unborn child falling from her stomach, persuaded the tall Plantagenet to call out in Norman-French, 'Laissez, Laissez'.

There is some controversy regarding the numbers killed over these two days. Some say 20,000; others as low as 7,000. We can only say that by far the greatest part of the population of Scotland's greatest town was slaughtered, and the town reduced to ruins.

While Edward Longshanks was surveying his handiwork, two Franciscan friars appeared with a letter, containing the information that Balliol was now renouncing his homage to this terrible monarch. 'Be it unto the fool, according to his folly', Edward was believed to have said. He proceeded to set his army on the march to the Scottish heartlands.

The main Scottish army gathered outside the town and fortress of Dunbar. The earl of the town was a strong supporter of Edward; his wife, one of the Comyn family, had handed over the castle to the Earls of Mar, Ross and Mentieth. Edward sent one his nobles, the Earl of Warenne, to besiege the fortress. Warenne duly invested the town, and was then told that there was a Scottish army coming to its relief. He took the main part of his army to meet the Scots at nearby Spottsmuir.

There is some confusion, even on the winning side, as to what happened next. According to most reports, Warenne led the army forward into a dip in the ground, which made the Scots think that the English were retreating. The Scottish advanced, and were met by the English army. Given that this must have been entirely a cavalry battle, the better armour and larger horses of the English must have been of greater use in close-quarter warfare than the hacks the Scottish were riding. The Scottish army promptly took off, and the garrison at Dunbar, seeing which way the wind was blowing, surrendered (Edward conveniently being on the scene for this second success). The earls and barons in the city were promptly sent down to London, and Edward went on what can only be described as a promenade through his new kingdom. Edinburgh surrendered after only five days of siege, while at Stirling, the castle was found to be almost deserted – the keys of the castle, in a rather anti-climactic incident, being handed over to the English and their king by the castle porter.

These defeats shattered whatever self-confidence the hapless Balliol might have had and, after wandering miserably through his kingdom, he surrendered to Edward's representatives at Kincardine, on 2 July. What happened next was a warning to anyone who might try and oppose Edward Longshanks: on 8 July, in Montrose, as Balliol handed over his kingdom to Edward, his royal insignia were taken and the royal surcoat was ripped from him – a colossal humiliation. Balliol was given the nickname 'Toom Tabard' (empty surcoat) by his subjects, who chose this savage appellation to describe their unwanted monarch.

Balliol was promptly sent south to the Tower of London, perhaps with a sigh of relief at quitting the land that had brought him so little joy. Edward, with typical thoroughness, collected the royal archives, regalia and treasures of Scotland, together with the coronation stone of Scone, which would remain under the coronation chair in Westminster Abbey until 1996, when it was sent back to its rightful home. Edward stayed at Berwick, re-establishing order in the city he had destroyed, and arranging for the administration of the land he had conquered with such ease. When Robert Bruce II requested that Edward make him king in return for his support, as promised, Edward is supposed to have answered in a rage, 'Have I nothing better to do than win kingdoms for you?', dismissing this contender to the throne almost as contemptuously as he had dismissed Balliol.

The victor of Dunbar, the Earl of Warenne, was made lieutenant of the kingdom, while the even more important post of treasurer was given to an obese cleric called Hugh de Cressingham. To make things official, Edward – who, as well as being a born killer, was a born bureaucrat – forced all the freeholders of Scotland to swear allegiance to him, by signing the famous 'Ragman role' acknowledging his right to Scotland. This meant, of course, that if they rebelled Edward would have documentary evidence that they had committed treason.

With the new kingdom, like the principality of Wales, now dangling from his belt, Edward was king of the whole of mainland Britain, achieving a feat that none of his forebears since the Saxon, Athelstan, had been able to accomplish. With typical arrogance, he was reported to have said on his return to England: 'Bon Besoigne fait qy do merde se deliver' ('he does good business who rids himself of shit').

The conquest of Scotland seemed so easy that Edward did not appear to care when his lieutenant, the Earl of Warenne, decided that the post was not to his liking, and that he would prefer to spend most of his time on his estates in Yorkshire. The corpulent Cressingham was left to administer the land of the broken northerners, and he has been accused, probably justly, of squeezing every penny he could out of his new viceroyalty.

13

The Wallace

At this time, there came to prominence perhaps the most enigmatic man ever to have been born in Scotland: William Wallace, whose fame has been guaranteed recently by the spate of books written about the Scottish wars and also, of course, by the film for which Mel Gibson, playing Wallace, scooped two Oscars.

It appears that William Wallace was the son of a petty knight, who was supposedly responsible for killing the Sheriff of Lanark in May 1297. Some say the sheriff had either raped or insulted his wife; others that Wallace's action was the first blow for freedom by a man appalled at the state of the land of his birth. (Wallace, incidentally, seems to mean Welshman: apparently a patriot does not have to have a native-sounding name). The scandal-hungry author of the *Lanercost Chronicle* states that the revolt, although headed by Wallace, whom he calls 'A chief of Brigands', was organised by James the Stewart and the ubiquitous Bishop Wishart of Glasgow. Taking into account the rather strange conduct of these men over the next few years, it is best to keep an open mind as to the reasons for the revolt.

What happened next, however, is fairly certain. Wallace marched upon the city of Scone at the head of an army composed mostly of the Scottish commons, and killed the justiciar who was holding courts there. He was joined by William 'The Bold', Lord of Douglas, who had been the not-very-effective governor of the citadel at Berwick during its siege.

With the Wallace and William Douglas now in Fife, a new character now enters the Scottish stage: Robert Bruce III, son of the
Earl of Carrick. This young man (he was only twenty-three at this
time) had been on the fringes of the Scottish scene for several years.
Like most of the nobility, he had sworn a personal oath to Edward,
and would have known very well what happened to people who
opposed Longshanks. He appears to have joined a group of Scottish
nobles at Irvine in western Scotland; this group were discussing, with
limited success, what to do about the state of Scotland and how to
deal with Wallace.

A very confused series of manoeuvres followed, none of which
pleased later historians of the nationalist school. It appears that
Edward sent a small army to oppose the Scots at Irvine, and the
English leaders offered a deal to the Bruce: he would get a pardon in
return for hostages. Bruce agreed, and Wishart and William Douglas
were put into English custody. (Douglas was imprisoned in Berwick,
where, not surprisingly, his behaviour was described as being 'savage
and abusive'. He was later sent to the Tower of London, where he
died.) The Wallace promptly marched north, to the land of Moray,
where he met a fellow-incendiary, Andrew Moray, who is said to
have fought at Dunbar. Moray appears to have been a man of far
greater wealth than Wallace, and if it had not been for his early death,
he might have had a far greater influence on Scottish affairs. He
managed to overthrow the English castles in the north with relative
ease, then, marching down south to Aberdeen, he linked up with
Wallace. They were subsequently joined by the Earl of Fife and other
desperadoes from the north.

This revolt appears to have been a genuinely popular movement,
which shows how much the common people hated the English.
Cressingham wrote home to Edward, describing the state of affairs
in frantic terms, and referring to the fact that many officials had
been murdered. Edward was unable to help to begin with, as he
was quarrelling with leading barons over the taxes he was raising
for his wars. With Edward helpless in London, Cressingham had to

depend on whatever local resources he could gather and on a levy of the northern nobles of England. In September 1297, therefore, a mostly English force gathered round the castle of Stirling, to oppose Wallace and Moray who, inconveniently, were stationed across the wide River Forth.

At this point Warenne deigned to put in an appearance, and joined Cressingham. The two armies appear to have numbered about 10,000 men each, with the English having the greater number of cavalry. On 9 and 10 September, two parleys took place – the civilised way to fight. With the English were the Earl of Lennox and the enigmatic James the Stewart. The two parleys achieved nothing, and may merely have been an excuse for various well-wishers south of the river to send information to the rebels concerning the English strength.

On 11 September, it was decided by common consent that a battle was to be fought, and early in the morning a party of infantry was sent over the bridge of the Forth, at Stirling. They were hastily called back when it was discovered that the Earl of Warenne was still asleep in his tent. Stirred from his slumbers, Warenne ordered Cressingham, a bellicose cleric if ever there was one, to advance over the bridge with a squadron of cavalry. A Scottish knight, Richard Lundie, pointed out that the bridge was so narrow that only two knights at a time could ride over the structure, and advised that he be given command of a force of men who could cross a nearby – and much wider – ford, in order to outflank the Scottish positions.

Cressingham, however, impatient at the delay, urged a direct advance. Warenne concurred, probably glad to get this egregious cleric away from him. Cressingham led the English cavalry across the bridge, where Wallace and Moray, with the finesse of snooker players potting a black, waited until a portion of the force had crossed the river, then launched the whole of their army in the attack. The English troops, mounted on their destriers, found themselves surrounded by swarms of foot soldiers wielding swords, axes and knives. In the marshy ground over the river, their lowborn opponents slaughtered the armoured knights like flies. On the south bank, Warenne looked

1 The scene of the battle of Byland. Note the steepness of the embankment up which the Scots advanced.

2 The ridge to the south of the English position at Byland. This is most likely the point at which the Scottish Highlanders flanked the English.

3 The hairpin bend on the road the Scots took on their way to attack the English at Byland. Note the steepness of the road up which the Scots advanced.

4 A picture of the *Gardes Ecosses* on the march. The Scottish army would have looked like this as it advanced at Byland.

5 The bridge at Myton, looking north-east. The Douglas and Moray would have had part of their army camped there.

6 Myton, looking south-west from the bridge. The English army would have marched over this area on their way to the unpleasant encounter.

7 The area immediately to the north-west of the bridge at Myton. This is where the Douglas and Moray would have been positioned, along with most of their army.

8 The bridge at Boroughbridge, looking due north. This would have been the point at which the English men-at-arms flanked the archers. It would have been a very hard position to attack at the best of times, and the bridge would have been much narrower then.

9 The bridge at Boroughbridge, from the south-east.

10 The river to the east of Boroughbridge. Once again, notice the steepness of the banks. With archers firing into them, Lancaster's knights would have found it almost impossible to cross the river here.

11 The castle at Pontefract, where Lancaster was tried and beheaded.

12 What the English would have faced at Myton. Utter chaos.

Left: 13 and *below*: 14 How elements of a Scottish schiltrom would have looked. The English would have faced formations like these at Bannockburn and Myton, and Lancaster would have faced something similar at Boroughbridge.

15 The plain of Stirling, looking west from the Wallace monument.

16 The killing fields of Stirling Bridge. The low-lying area to the left of the picture is where the Wallace slaughtered the English knights in 1296.

17 The north face of the rock at Edinburgh. This was the place the Earl of Moray led his men to take the castle in 1313. They had to climb this rock at night, carrying arms and armour.

18 A long shot of the same crag. It can be seen that the feat accomplished by Moray and his men was incredible.

19 The north wall of the city of Berwick.

20 Durham Cathedral.

21 The south-eastern walls of Berwick, with the river Tweed in the background.

22 The gatehouse of Carlisle. The heads of Edward I's enemies would have been spiked there.

23 The castle of Carlisle from the south.

24 and 25 The keep at Carlisle.

on in horror as his men were killed before his eyes. One knight, Sir Marmaduke Tweng, was reported to have hacked his way through the ranks of Scots and retreated over the bridge. Cressingham was killed in battle. His skin, according to the Lanercost chronicler, was stripped from his body, to be used as a scabbard by the Scots. Wallace, of course, was given the blame for this. Considering discretion to be the better part of valour, Warenne proceeded to turn and gallop off the battlefield, leaving his army to shift for itself.

The patriotic feelings of the Earl of Lennox and the Stewart were suddenly aroused at this point and, with that eye to the main chance which was so lacking in the descendants of the Stewart, they led their men to plunder the English baggage. Meanwhile, Warenne was reputed to have galloped all the way from Stirling to Berwick in one day. Not altogether surprisingly, his horse foundered on arrival, and was rumoured 'never to have ate corn again'!

The English presence in Scotland now being non-existent, Wallace proceeded to lead his troops down into an invasion of the East March of England. October and November saw a riot of plundering and slaughter, with the Scots deciding to give their southern neighbours a dose of Longshanks's own medicine. Honour being satisfied, they retired with their booty; their betters were left with the problem of how to deal with these lowborn champions. This problem was exacerbated a few months later when Moray died, leaving Wallace in splendid isolation at the top of the feudal heap.

In March 1298, at a rather bemused meeting in Ettrick Forest, Wallace was appointed sole guardian of the realm, a rather strange position since none of the nobles seemed to have the slightest intention of obeying him. One of them had either the foresight or the irony to knight Wallace, which at least gave him a social rank that meant he could speak to his betters. But his hour would be brief: by making peace with the king of France, and by giving in to some of the demands of his own earls, Edward had gathered an army to march north, and he intended to give the Scots and their obstreperous leader a lesson they would never forget.

Leading an army over 15,000 strong, including for apparently the first time a group of men armed with the dreaded longbow, Edward marched into the northern kingdom at the beginning of July. The countryside, either due to a deliberate scorched-earth policy or to the fact that two armies had ravaged it in as many years, was now a desert, from which no supplies could be plundered. As they advanced, the army proceeded to slowly starve. Eventually some supply ships made an appearance, but they carried only wine. The effects of spirituous liquors on empty stomachs are only too well known, and soon many of the troops were rolling drunk and fighting with each other.

The army, which had marched unopposed from Berwick to beyond Edinburgh, seemed to be in a position of almost complete collapse, when the pro-English Earl of Dunbar told the Plantaganet king that the Scots were encamped nearby at Falkirk. The English army seemed to regain its discipline almost immediately. On the night of 21 July, the king lay among his men like a common foot soldier (incurring two broken ribs when a disrespectful horse walked over him). Morning broke to reveal that the Wallace had organised his army with the infantry in the centre, in one line of three or four great schiltroms (circles of spearmen), and the cavalry, made up of disgruntled nobles, on the flanks or at the rear.

The Scottish army was about 14,000 strong – great in numbers, but short on trust. According to some reports, Robert Bruce III was on the English side at this conflict, while according to other reports the Wallace had been forced by his rumbustious followers to accept battle, against his better judgement.

If this was the case, Wallace's hesitation is understandable. The battle opened when Edward ordered the left wing of his cavalry, under the command of the Earls of Norfolk, Hereford and Lincoln, to circle to the west, and the right wing, under the Bishop of Durham, the bellicose Anthony Bek, to circle east. The two wings took their positions and charged the Scots. The schiltroms drove them off, but the Scottish cavalry fled. Some have seen this as an example of the treacherous behaviour of the Scottish nobles, who left their less well-born comrades in the lurch. It was probably due more to the fact that the Scottish cavalry was hopelessly outnumbered, and their men far less strongly armoured than their English counterparts.

Whatever the reason, the infantry found themselves isolated. Cavalry attacks from the rear, combined with a hail of missiles, broke the shield ring and allowed the armoured cavalry of England to erupt into the ranks of the Scottish infantry, and slaughter their presumptuous foes. Several thousand men died in a battle that destroyed the power, but not the legend, of the Wallace.

The victory at Falkirk, however, solved nothing. Edward, unable to feed his army, had to lead his troops back across the Lothian to more fertile English pastures. The Scots now found they had got *de facto* independence, albeit at a terrible price, and they had to come up with a means of governing their country. A compromise agreement was reached when John Comyn, son of the Earl of Buchan and nephew of the absent Balliol, and Robert Bruce III, Earl of Carrick, who shall now be known as the Bruce, were appointed as joint guardians of the kingdom in 1298. The Wallace was now a figure of no importance, reduced to going on diplomatic jaunts to gain the support of uninterested foreign potentates.

The next two years would see little fighting, except for the inevitable border skirmishes. More unpleasant violence would be seen at a meeting in August 1299 at Peebles, where the various Scottish factions met to discuss what to do next. The Comyn faction suspected, on good authority, that Bruce had been canvassing the help of Malcolm Wallace, William's brother, and the Bishop of St Andrew's, William Lamberton – who had been appointed, as one of his last acts, by William Wallace – in order to have the Bruce declared king. The resulting quarrel exploded into a fistfight, and only the intervention of the Stewart stopped this brawl from becoming a miniature battle.

With the Bruce/Lamberton faction and the Comyn/Balliol faction at loggerheads, the kingdom could only wait with trepidation for the next invasion of Edward I. This duly came in 1300, in a campaign that, to the disgust of the chroniclers but to the probable delight of the commons, ended in the capture of Caerlaverock Castle in the south-west, and very little else.

The only other important event that occurred at this time was the fact that the Pope of the day, Boniface VIII, demanded that Balliol be surrendered into his custody, and that Edward give him some justification concerning the rights of overlordship he claimed in Scotland. Edward allowed the Balliol to go to France, and proceeded to send the Pope a letter of great length, containing some very dubious reasoning as to why he should be the lord paramount of Scotland. He did not, of course, pay any attention to the Pope's demand that he cease interfering in Scottish affairs.

Another invasion of Scotland, in which Edward was accompanied by his heir, the seventeen-year-old Edward of Caernarvon, achieved greater success. By careful logistical means, Edward slowly advanced into the heart of southern Scotland, where he was probably joined by the Bruce, who had changed sides again (the Bruce's estates were almost all in the south-west, i.e. the areas nearest to any English invasion). Various meetings of delegates from the Comyn faction were unsuccessful, and only the fact that Edward was again faced with war with France prevented Edward from re-staking his claim to the Scottish throne.

By 1303, however, Edward was free from the war with France and able to mount yet another campaign in Scotland. This time, with a fairly loyal kingdom behind him and a divided kingdom opposing him, Edward managed to overcome the southern part of Scotland and march to the lands of Buchan, in the north-east of Scotland. The Comyns, aware that the power of Longshanks was almost limitless, agreed to terms, and by the middle of 1304 a series of agreements was hammered out: in effect, Edward gave the Scots a form of home rule. An English governor was to rule a land where the Scots would run their own affairs and the major offices of the land were to be given to Scots, although the sheriffdoms of the most important cities, such as Edinburgh, would remain in English hands. This was a most remarkable agreement coming from a king known in his later years for his savagery, and a people known for their disunity. For two years, there was relative peace in the land.

In August 1305, the Wallace was captured in Glasgow, not by means of great deeds of arms and chivalry, but owing to a bribe given to one Ralph de Halliburton, who betrayed him to the Sheriff of Glasgow. Wallace was taken to London to endure the full traitor's death: drawn through the streets, hanged while half dead, castrated, disembowelled and beheaded. His body was quartered and sent to strategic locations in Scotland, so the Scots could see what would happen to those who opposed Edward Longshanks. Though accused of treason, Wallace steadfastly refused to beg for mercy, saying that as he had not given homage to Edward, how could he be a traitor to him?

Though other heroes may have been better born, left a greater degree of fame and had more books published about them, the true hero of the wars of the English and the Scots is the Wallace. For a brief hour, he raised a group of men to follow him in the cause of pure freedom, opposing a tyrannical and imperialist foreign power.

14

Dumfries

The prospect of Edward now being able to ignore Scottish affairs proved a pipe dream. Though peace had returned to the Scots, tolerance had not. As meetings were held in the various palaces of the area, Bruce found out that the powerful Comyn clan were slowly freezing him out of the affairs of state. Sheriffdoms held by his family for generations were lost, leaving the Bruce to imagine what would happen to him when Edward, now in his mid-sixties and visibly ailing, would leave this land and start conquering the lands of the otherworld.

It was probably to complain about the state of affairs, or to try to do a deal with him, that the Bruce called John Comyn, heir-presumptive of the Comyn clan, to see him at Dumfries Abbey in February 1306. What happened next is one of the most famous but also one of the most peculiar events in Scottish history. On 10 February, at the Church of the Grey Friars, the Bruce and his supporters killed the Comyn and one of the Comyn's relatives at the high altar, leading to the revolt which enabled the Bruce to be crowned king of the Scots and drive the English from Scotland.

We have a number of accounts as to why the murder occurred, accounts which must be treated with caution, as they are all either pro- or anti-Bruce. The pro-Bruce chroniclers state that the two men had done a deal, whereby the Bruce agreed to give the Comyn his lands in return for his support for the kingship when Edward died. This agreement was ratified by means of a sealed indenture. The Bruce was then ordered by Edward to come to England to attend a Parliament. Edward was informed by sources coming from the Comyn that the Bruce was going to betray him; he asked the Bruce if this was true, and the Bruce replied with quips and jests to assuage the king's suspicions. In his lodgings that night, he received a messenger from his friend Ralph de Monthermer, Earl of Gloucester, bearing twelve silver pence and a pair of spurs: an oblique warning that the Bruce had better flee for his life.

Accompanied by his clerk, the Bruce fled London, reaching the Scottish-English border a few days later. Near the city of Carlisle, he met one of the Comyn's attendants. He forced the man to give up his possessions, killing him when he refused. On him was a letter to Edward, telling him of the agreement and urging the execution of the Bruce. In a rage, the Bruce met his family at Lochmaben, told them of what had happened, and called the Comyn to meet him at Dumfries. He showed the Comyn the letter, accused him of betrayal and, when the Comyn was unrepentant, slew him at the altar of the abbey.

With all respect to the followers and later historians of the Bruce, this story does not make sense. To begin with, there was no Parliament called for that year and, furthermore, there is no evidence that the Bruce was in London or any part of England at this time. For the Comyn to agree to the Bruce becoming king is also frankly incredible: the Comyn was the nephew of Balliol, the old king of the Scots, and was, by his own standards, nearer to the line of the throne than the Bruce was. To agree to the Bruce becoming king would be to shatter everything he and his clan had fought for over the years.

It should also be pointed out that there is no evidence of the existence of the letter or the indenture, and there is no evidence that Edward sent out any orders for the Bruce to be stopped on his ride out of London. The death of the messenger on the Scottish border is another problem. Is it likely that the Bruce, riding for his life, should quite by accident meet the Comyn's man, bearing a letter recommending his execution? This is too lucky a meeting to really be given any credibility at all, so the story of the Bruce holding out the Comyn's letter at Dumfries must also be called into question.

The manner of the meeting at the Grey Friars is also rather strange. According to one chronicler, the Englishman Thomas Grey, the Bruce knew the Comyn was residing at the nearby castle of Dalswinton, and ordered some of his brothers, who were residing at Lochmaben at the time, to go there and slay him. As an Englishman, whose father was captured at Bannockburn in 1314, and who himself would later become a prisoner of the Scots, Grey's story is necessarily rather suspect. He claims that the Bruce's brothers duly went to Dalswinton, where they found the Comyn in such an easygoing and friendly mood that they could not bring themselves to kill him. The Bruce said angrily when they returned, 'You are right lazy, let me kill him.'

Our other source is the famous history written by John Barbour, a fourteenth-century cleric, who is responsible for many of the stories about the Bruce and his paladin, James Douglas. Barbour says quite bluntly that the Bruce went to Dumfries Abbey, showed the Comyn the indenture, and 'then with a knife, reft his life'. Taking into account the fact that Barbour's history is on the whole a magnificent piece of propaganda for Robert the Bruce, this lack of explanation as to the slaying of the Comyn is very revealing. If Barbour knew of any other reasons the Bruce had for the murder, he would have put them down in his chronicle: his silence in this matter speaks volumes.

The actual slaying itself is of interest. The Comyn appears to have come to the abbey accompanied by only one follower, named as either Alexander Comyn or his uncle, Robert. One chronicler states that when the Bruce stabbed the Comyn with his dagger, Comyn's kinsman drew his sword and slashed at the Bruce, who was not harmed because he was wearing armour under his clothes. The Bruce's retinue then slew the man. This story seems to show that the Bruce had entered the town of Dumfries with a large retinue, whereas the Comyns had come on their own.

What on earth are we to deduce from this evidence? The fact that neither the letter nor the indenture have been found is extremely suspicious, ruling out the idea that there was a long-drawn-out plan to divide the realm. Barbour's failure to explain the Bruce's actions is also very strange. His work, after all, is supposed to be a hagiography of the Bruce. The size of the Bruce's retinue and the absence of one for the Comyns is also of interest.

A possible explanation is that the Bruce was planning to stage a *coup* against the English administration when the visibly ailing Edward should die. He knew he could not do this without the help of the Comyn clan. As he had been repeatedly sidelined by both Edward and the Comyns, he realised that in the near future he and his family would be in danger, so he called the Comyn in order to suggest that he help him in claiming the throne. The Comyn, shocked at an idea that would have meant his family giving up what they considered to be their rightful claim to the throne, and understanding that an outbreak of war could result, refused, either with rage or disbelief. The Bruce, whose early life had shown him to be a somewhat immature individual, completely lost control of himself and killed the Comyn.

Whether this is to be described as murder or manslaughter is open to question. In this day and age the Bruce would certainly have been found guilty of at least the latter, and the behaviour of him and his men immediately after the killing of the Comyn is even more suspicious. Straight after the slaying, the Bruce and his entourage rode to the castle of Dumfries. This was immediately surrendered to the Bruce by its keeper, Sir Richard Girard. The king's justices, sitting in the great hall, had to be threatened with having the building burned down in front of them before they would surrender to the Bruce.

Over the next few days, the nearby castles of Dalswinton and Tibbers were seized, as were fortresses in the west of Scotland, allowing the Bruce to maintain contact with both the Isles to the west, and also the earldom of Ulster in Ireland (the Bruce's second wife, Elizabeth de Burgh, was the daughter of the Lord of Ulster, Richard de Burgh). The speed with which he managed to accomplish these feats is rather strange, and seems to show that at the very least he was planning to stage a *coup d'état* when Edward died. The next little incident is also rather odd: the Bruce had killed in the sacred precincts of a church and had committed sacrilege. He therefore needed absolution for his sins. He rode to Glasgow, to Bishop Wishart, and confessed his sins; Wishart thereupon gave him absolution, and brought from the treasury of the cathedral the royal standard, which had been hidden since the reign of Alexander III, together with some rich robes for the king to wear at his coronation ceremony. Some cynics have seen this as proof that the death of the Comyn was cold-blooded murder, with Wishart acting as an accessory; others say it was an example of the Scottish Church anointing one who would liberate it from the English monarchy, and from the hated demand of the Archbishop of Canterbury that all churches in the British Isles should be his subjects. Whatever the reason, the Bruce received absolution, along with oaths of fealty from nearby churchmen and nobles, and rode to Scone to be officially enthroned as king of the Scots.

On his way to the coronation, he met a young man aged about twenty-two, riding a splendid horse, who offered him his fealty. This encounter would be one of the most remarkable in history: Robert de Bruce, the *de facto* king of the Scots, had met his greatest paladin, James of Douglas, known as the Black Douglas.

15

The Bruce and the Douglas

The Bruce and the Douglas, if not the two greatest men of the race of the Scots, are among the most famous. The future liberator, Robert the Bruce, was born on 11 July 1274, at the castle belonging to his father, the Earl of Carrick, at Turnberry. As the eldest son of one of the great lords of Scotland, he was born into a very select elite. He would have grown up expecting deference and obedience, even from men far older than him. The fact that he was born in the west of Scotland is quite interesting. At this time, Scotland in effect was a kingdom of three languages: the courtly Norman French spoken by the elite, the northern English dialect, soon to be called Lowland Scots, spoken by the mass of the people, and the Gaelic tongue spoken on the west coast and in the Western Isles. The Bruce grew up trilingual almost from birth, which accounts for his ability to communicate with ease with the subjects of his future kingdom – a factor which would be very important in the coming years.

His education would have been the normal one for the times, in that he would have served as a page and squire in a noble household, perhaps the household of his grandfather, Robert Bruce I. Here he would have learned the basic skills of the nobility, how to serve and assist his lord at his table, how to dance and make polite conversation. There is no doubt that the Bruce had a considerable amount of scholastic learning as well, since it is mentioned by several chroniclers that he enjoyed reading. Taking into account the fact that Latin at the time was the international language of the Church, and used in nearly all legal documents, there is a good chance that the Bruce would have had an understanding of this tongue as well. The main training he would have undertaken, however, was to learn how to ride, hunt and use the weapons of the day. In these, the Bruce must have been a quite remarkable practitioner. If only a few of the stories told about him are true, the Bruce must have been a ferocious fighting man and superb horseman. In not one of the combats was he bested, and he was able to ride and fight with the best of his men until well into his fifties. He would have been brought up with the idea that he was the rightful heir to the throne of the Scots. The driving force he displayed to achieve his goal shows just how determined, or how desperate, he was.

The early years of the Bruce, the ones following the accession of Balliol, seem to show a man being dragged about in the wake of events, and dominated by his grandfather. The death of his powerful grandfather in 1295 seemed to leave him adrift for several years, the ambiguity of his behaviour regarding the rise of the Wallace being a moot point here. The death in 1304 of his father, to whom he does not seem to have been very close, put him in the forefront of affairs, and the fact that he was frozen out of the administration of the kingdom seems to show that he was regarded as something of a political lightweight.

Realising this, the Bruce arranged for his meeting with the Comyn in 1306. He knew that when Edward died the Comyn faction would have a free hand in governing the realm, and the future of his own family would be very vulnerable. The murder/manslaughter of Comyn put him beyond the pale as far as that clan was concerned. The death of the heir to one of the most powerful earldoms in Scotland, together with an uncle of the same clan, made it a matter of honour for the Comyns to call for a blood feud.

The reaction of Edward of England was also to be feared. Edward, though old, was by no means a fool, and the Bruce knew that when information reached him about the meeting at Dumfries and the death of the Comyn, the king would realise that they had not gathered there to discuss the state of the weather. Even in the fourteenth century, an age inured to violence, the killing of an earl's son together with his uncle would cause a scandal. Edward would put two and two together and realise that the Bruce was planning, if not a revolt, than a *coup* after his death.

The Bruce now had to face the fact that one of the most powerful clans in Scotland was going to launch a blood feud against him, and that the terrible king of England was about to attack him with all his might. From this time on, the Bruce seems to have become a new character: more determined, clear-headed and decisive. The man he had met on the way to Scone would be his greatest weapon in his struggles with the English, and James Douglas would find in the Bruce a man who would help him fulfil his own destiny.

Born in about the year 1286, at the castle of Douglas in central Scotland, James appears in his early years to have followed the normal life of a son born to the Scottish gentry. The real change occurred when his father was incarcerated in the dungeons of the Tower of London, and James was sent for his own protection to Paris, to forestall him being seized as a hostage. This enforced stay gave him the opportunity to live among slum children, make friends very quickly – he was known for his ability to get along with people of any rank or degree – and to learn the ethics of gang warfare among a group of children who knew nothing about the laws of chivalry.

James came back to Scotland in about 1299, in the household of William Lamberton, the new Bishop of St Andrews. Lamberton most likely brought to James the news of his father's death, and the further news that Edward had disinherited him, giving James's inheritance to one of his favourite hitmen, Robert de Clifford, Lord of Skipton. The news of the death and of his disinheritance must have come as a shock to the young boy, but a position in Lamberton's household gave him the opportunity to learn the techniques of administration and the law, as well as a bird's-eye view on how the affairs of Scotland were progressing in the last years of the thirteenth century.

The defining incident in James's life appears to have been in 1304, when he was taken to the great camp of Edward I, near the castle of Stirling. Here Lamberton begged a favour of the redoubtable Plantagenet, and asked him to return his father's estates to James. Edward flatly refused: the son of the man who had joined Wallace, and who had helped the Wallace inflict the most terrible military defeat of the time on Edward's soldiers, be given back his land? Never! Lamberton hustled the youth away from Longshanks. The Hammer of the Scots had just seen, for a brief moment, the Hammer of the English.

It was while the Bishop was at Berwick that news came that the Bruce was about to make a claim for the throne. It would have come as a revelation to the young James, wondering if he was to spend the rest of his life as a pensioner in the Bishop's household. He begged and received permission to join the Bruce, and indeed Lamberton allowed him to ride his own palfrey, Ferrand.

He said to James that he could take the horse, and that if the groom of the stable saw him, he could deal with him appropriately. James saddled the palfrey; the groom saw what was happening, tried to stop James taking the Bishop's own mount, and was struck down for his pains. Barbour, who relates this anecdote, does so quite cheerfully, which shows how unimportant he considered the unwashed multitude in comparison with the affairs of the day.

The most unusual factor about the story of the Douglas is that Barbour provides us with a physical description of the man who would soon become the terror of the northern shires of England: he had black hair; his face was rather grey; he was tall, broad-shouldered and lithe. His manners, it appears, were very good, and he spoke with a lisp. He appears to have been generally very polite to both high and low, an uncommon accomplishment in the early fourteenth century, which seems to be one of the reasons why he was able to lead his men by both example and inspiration.

The Bruce and the Douglas met on the way to Scone; James knelt and did homage; the Bruce acknowledged this, listened courteously to his story and allowed him to join his entourage. Thus was born the greatest partnership in the history of the Scots.

On 25 March 1306, less than two months since the killing of the Comyn, the Bruce was officially enthroned at Scone: the descendant of Malcolm Canmore, Macbeth and Kenneth Macalpin. At the ceremony, there occurred one of the most famous incidents of the Scottish Middle Ages. Since time immemorial, it had been the privilege of the Earls of Fife to lead the king of the Scots to be enthroned at Scone. The Earl at this time was a minor held in the custody of Edward I (who possibly kept him there to avoid precisely this situation). To the delight of everyone, Isabel Macduff, the sister of the Earl of Fife, came to Scone to take the place of her brother and lead the Bruce to his coronation. What made this event so strange and romantic is that Isabel was married to the son of the Comyn, Earl of Buchan, and was therefore related by marriage to the slain Comyn himself. This event gave cachet to the coronation, provided poets and nationalists with the chance to warble about the ideal of patriotism overcoming the calling of family, and ultimately ensure that the lady in question would suffer a terrible fate.

When Edward at last heard of the death of the Comyn and the coronation of the Bruce, his rage was terrible. Whether it was fury at having being fooled (as he saw it), whether it was seeing his life's work crumble, whether it was the fact that he had been betrayed by someone who had sworn allegiance to him, or whether he simply realised that he was going to another place soon, and was determined to ensure this young hooligan got what he deserved, Edward plunged into a merciless vendetta of the kind he had never initiated before, and gave orders with a savagery and vindictiveness more appropriate for a Mafia chief of Sicily than the ruler of a Christian kingdom.

The Earl of Pembroke, Aylmer de Valence, was ordered to march north to deal with the revolt as best he could. Edward and his son, Edward, Prince of Wales, would follow with the levies of the kingdom. A barrage of letters demanding information, commanding that the estates of the rebels be seized, and ordering that all the rebels be put to death, showered on Pembroke's head. The dragon banner was ordered to be unfurled: a symbol, if it was needed, that Edward would give no quarter in the conflict that followed.

Within weeks the rebellious churchmen, Wishart and Lamberton, were taken. Only their clerical rank stopped them from being executed, and this would not be the case a few weeks later, as Edward became more vindictive than ever. Both sides now appeared to want a battle: the Bruce to show he was worthy of his throne, and Pembroke to show Edward that he was no Earl of Warenne and to stop the hail of letters showering on his head. At Perth, in June 1306, the two sides approached one other. On 18 June, Pembroke and his army, ensconced behind the walls of Perth, saw the Bruce and his army line up outside the walls of the city and, in true medieval style, offer battle. As it was a Sunday, Valence replied that it would be sacrilege to fight on such a holy day, but that he would fight tomorrow.

The Bruce brought his army away and encamped at Methven, six miles away. His men stripped their armour, unsaddled their horses and caught up on some sleep, which made them very easy targets that night when Pembroke and his army attacked them. In the chaos that followed, only the presence of his brother-in-law, Sir Christopher Seton, an English knight who beat off the attack of Sir Philip Mowbray, stopped the Bruce from being killed or captured. The Scottish camp dissolved in rout, many being captured or slain. The rest of the army fled into the hills. The surprise at Methven was a salutary lesson for the Bruce. It was an even greater one for the Douglas. For the rest of his life, he would have a concern for scouting and watching for ambushes which, by the standards of the time, seemed to verge on a mania.

The Bruce's forlorn group of followers proceeded to march west through the Highlands to the Western Isles, where he was related to the lords of the area. Crossing the lands of Lorn, they were ambushed again by a pro-Comyn force, the Macdougals of Lorne, at Dalry. The Bruce showed his training and background by killing three men with three strokes of his sword, and managing to get his battered company past this new enemy. Faced with the complete dissolution of his band, he then took a decision that must have caused him anguish for years: he decided to send away his wife and womenfolk – including Isabel Macduff, who would not have been human if she were not thinking she had made a terrible mistake in crowning the Bruce – to Moray in the north-east, where they could hopefully take a ship to Norway, where the Bruce's sister was queen. The women, accompanied by the Bruce's brother Nigel and the Earl of Atholl, rode away, leaving the little band of supporters to march on foot to the west.

The tale of the Bruce's life over the next few months is one of hardship and determination. Journeying to the Western Isles, he took refuge on the Isle of Rathlin off the coast of Ireland. He then sailed to the west coast of Scotland, landed there, and launched a guerrilla campaign, regarded as a textbook example of irregular warfare. By means of ambushes, raids and assassinations, he soon managed to regain lands in the west.

He must have been encouraged by the fact that if he was captured no mercy would be given to him. As the Bruce proceeded to harry the English in the west of Scotland, he received terrible news almost daily: the Earl of Ross had captured the ladies of the court, who had taken sanctuary in Tain, in the north of Scotland. His queen and daughter were sent to England, to be incarcerated far away from their husband and father. His sister Mary and the unfortunate Isabel of Buchan were punished in a way specially devised by Edward, one which shocked even his own son. Isabel Macduff was sent to Berwick, Mary Bruce to Roxburgh. Here they were imprisoned in cages: their only privacy was the right to a privy. Christian de Bruce, another sister, was also imprisoned.

Nigel Bruce was dead; he was captured in Kildrummy Castle, when a traitor burned down the grain store. The traitor was promised a great deal of gold for this feat, which was given to him in molten form and poured down his throat. Nigel Bruce was hanged at Berwick. Christopher Seton, the man who had saved the Bruce's life at Methven, was taken at Lochdoon Castle. As an English knight, there is no doubt that he was a traitor according to the lights of the time, so he was hanged, drawn and quartered at Carlisle. Simon Fraser, who had fought with both the Wallace and the Comyns against Edward and been captured at Methven, was sent to London, where his head soon joined that of Wallace over London Bridge.

Two of the Bruce's other brothers had been caught: Thomas, the youngest, and Alexander, a cleric. They were among the most brilliant scholars of their time, and were executed in Carlisle. The Earl of Atholl, who had left with the Bruce women, managed to reach the sea and tried to escape by galley. He was caught by an English ship and sent to London. A problem arose here: he was a great peer of the realm and distantly related to Edward himself, being the descendant of one of the numerous bastards of King John, Edward's grandfather. It was pointed out to Edward by his second wife, Margaret of France, that an earl and a relative of Edward himself could not be treated like a common criminal. Edward agreed, and gave Atholl an uncommon death. In honour of his Plantaganet blood, he was permitted to ride a white horse to the gallows, which had been built thirty feet high. The ailing Edward was supposed to have been delighted when told of Atholl's death.

These terrible setbacks forced the Bruce to fight to the death every day. By ambushes, feints and stratagems, he managed to reclaim the western area of Scotland. The ageing Edward, enraged at this temerity, rose from his sickbed and moved painfully to Carlisle, where he was to spend his time sending furious letters to his lords, urging the destruction of the Bruce. His temper could not have been improved by the news coming in of James Douglas. Leading only two men to his ancestral castle of Douglas, he greeted his tenants, whom he would not have seen for over ten years. On 19 March, Palm Sunday, he and the villagers attacked the garrison of Douglas while they were celebrating mass. He afterwards went to the castle and dined on the meal the garrison's cook had prepared for them. He then had the survivors of the garrison beheaded in the castle cellar, and the castle plundered and burned. This episode of the 'Douglas Larder' was the first of the sagas concerning James Douglas. By the use of secrecy and surprise, he had slaughtered his enemies. Twice more, by means of ambush, he would lure the garrison of Douglas out of the walls, and twice he would slaughter those thus enticed.

These unchivalrous antics on the part of the Scottish hooligans enraged Edward to such a point that he decided to lead a force himself to destroy the Bruce. In July, he had himself hauled into the saddle to march into the land he had almost hammered into submission. The effort was too much even for the most formidable of the Plantagenets: on 7 July, Edward I, king of England, Lord of Ireland, Duke of Aquitaine, Lord Paramount of Scotland, died in the arms of his servants.

In his own way, the king had acted according to the standards of the time. The fact that he had not managed to conquer the fractious people of the north was due to his being unable to carry on the conquest to its logical end. It was said that when the death of the mighty king was reported to the Bruce and his followers, they cried with sheer relief. They knew the man who had tried to dominate their land for so long was gone. The Bruce, at least, realised that the man who would succeed Edward as king would not be so great an adversary.

16

Edward II

For centuries, historians have blamed Edward II, son of the Hammer of the Scots, for leaving the northern shires so swiftly and hurrying to London to arrange for his coronation. This is an unfair criticism: he had to get back to London as soon as he could so he could officially take over the role of his father. He paid the correct honours to his father's body, and arranged for it to be sent for burial in Westminster Abbey, where it still lies, under an impressive weight of stone.

But from the very beginning, the chroniclers appear to have been disturbed at the ascension of this strange creature. Born on 25 April 1284, Edward was the only one of the brood of sons produced by Eleanor of Castile to survive into adulthood. He must hardly have known his mother and father, due to his father's habit of travelling throughout his lands and fighting the Welsh, and his mother's death in 1290. This may account for the distinct lack of affection between father and son in Edward II's early years.

His boyhood tutor, Guy Ferrer, appears to have had a lot on his hands with this boy. Edward would go on to display a markedly strange choice of pastimes as he matured. He enjoyed music, hunting and gambling, not strange in any royal household before or since, but also loved the more unusual activities of hedging and thatching. As well as failing to discourage these very odd habits, Ferrer appears to have been notably unsuccessful in another matter: that of encouraging the future heir of the throne to do a little work. In marked contrast to his father, whom none could accuse of not taking his role seriously, the new king would show himself, quite simply, to be bone idle, disliking any notion that he had a duty to his kingdom.

It appears to have been obvious to his father that the son he had sired was not made of the stuff required to be a king of the English. There are several incidents mentioned in the chronicles of the time that testify to the tensions between father and son. The most famous concerns Edward II's love for Piers Gaveston, a Gascon knight.

Edward is generally accepted to have been a homosexual, in an age which regarded this as being a crime against God. After having had a number of disputes with his father about the expensive way he ran his household, he had met Gaveston at about the age of seventeen, when the Gascon was appointed a knight of his household. Gaveston appeared to have a great deal of the braggadocio associated with southern France, and his confident, outgoing manner must have come as a breath of fresh air to a son whose father was a very overpowering and critical presence. A homosexual relationship probably resulted, which must have made the old king more than a little concerned at his heir's behaviour. In the winter of 1306, Edward asked his father to grant Ponthieu, a large lordship in France, to Gaveston.

'You wretched bastard!' the old king was reputed to have said (a totally unfounded attack on the virtue of his first wife Eleanor, the Infanta of Castile). 'Do you want to give lands away now? You who never gained any? As God loves, if not for a fear of breaking up the kingdom you should never enjoy your inheritance!' Just to make sure he had got the point, Edward *père* proceeded to tear out tufts of hair from his son's head, before ordering him from the room. With a father such as this, there is no wonder tension existed between the two. Edward ordered Gaveston to be exiled from England, not so much through fear that the relationship was inappropriate as to make his son wake up and stand on his own two feet.

His father's death must have come as a relief to Edward II, and he showed this by immediately ordering Gaveston back from exile. If this move could be excused as that of a young man wanting to banish the shadow of a formidable father, what happened next was regarded as quite shocking; even modern-day apologists have not found anything creditable or even vaguely intelligent in Edward's actions. He made Gaveston Earl of Cornwall, one of the richest earldoms in the kingdom, and married him off to his own niece, Margaret, daughter of the Earl of Gloucester. This was regarded as scandalous: the younger son of a petty knight of Gascony was now one of the peers of the realm and, by marriage, the king's nephew.

What happened next was even more ominous. Edward left for France to marry the French king's daughter, Isabelle, leaving Gaveston the regent of the kingdom in his absence. More than one chronicler was aghast at this, and the coronation, which took place on 25 February 1308, made things even worse. Gaveston, to the fury of the other lords, was given the task of carrying the crown of St Edward, which meant he preceded the king to the throne. His dress was believed to be more splendid than the king's: indeed, it was stated that he dressed 'more like the God Mars than a mortal man'.

The French lords who accompanied Isabelle were enraged to see Edward treat her with contempt, seeming to have eyes only for Gaveston. Part of the walls of the cathedral collapsed, the banquet was badly organised, and the coronation ended with the French lords leaving in a state of anger and bewilderment. Isabelle felt humiliated, and many chroniclers bewailed the fact that the king had not conducted himself in the way expected of a king of the English.

Edward's actions have been excused as those of a young man recently freed from the constraints of his father's disapproval, especially bearing in mind that the fourteenth century had different ideas from the twenty-first as to appropriate standards of behaviour. This apologia, however, ignores the evidence that can be gleaned from reading the chronicles of the time: the men and women who saw Edward close at hand, and who had dealings with him, realised very quickly that the man they were facing just did not fulfil what was expected of a king of the time. Favouritism, low-born pastimes and sexual misconduct could be excused, if the man had tried to act like a king. But this, as has been pointed out by modern historians, Edward failed to do. He was a very lazy and not particularly intelligent man, who had no interest in ruling, changed his mind from day to day, was regarded as bad-mannered and allowed his favourites to rule in his name. It is noticeable that although other English kings who were regarded as failures, such as Richard III or Henry VI, have had their defenders – and indeed their reputations have been considerably enhanced – the reputation of Edward, along with that of Henry V, Richard the Lionheart and William of Normandy, has gone down even lower than the one he possessed at the time.

It is not surprising that the Scots, at the news of the death of the dreaded father, would weep with relief, knowing the son would not be so formidable an enemy. They were quite right.

17

1307–1314:
From Rebellion to
Conquest

Considering that Edward's obsession with Gaveston nearly brought the kingdom of England to the brink of civil war on several occasions, it is hardly surprising that Edward could not pay much attention to Scottish affairs. It is even less surprising that Bruce and his followers took advantage of the opportunity to reconquer their lands.

They were greatly helped in this by the fact that Edward reduced the amount of help sent to his men in Scotland, with the result that the Bruce, who showed a genius for guerrilla warfare, managed by means of small-scale battles such as Glen Trool, the Pass of Brander and Loudon Hill to occupy most of south-west Scotland. In the winter of 1307, the Bruce was able to make his famous march through the Great Glen, into the heartlands of the earldom of Buchan, and there he ravaged the north-east of Scotland to such a degree that it required another fifty years for it to recover. The Comyns were defeated at the battle of Inverurie on 23 May 1308, and the Bruce could now begin to call himself the king of the Scots.

By the end of the summer of that year, only three towns north of the Tay remained in the hands of the English or their adherents:

Perth, Banff and Dundee. It should be pointed out that Edward tried to campaign in Scotland at this time, but was unable to do so owing to the fact that the great lord of the land expressly refused to help the king while Gaveston was around, accusing the Gascon, with good reason, of being offensive personally and dangerous politically.

It was only in September 1310, quite late in the campaigning season, that Edward was able to lead an army into southern Scotland, and then he was only able to march around the kingdom south of the Clyde, strengthening his fortresses. The Bruce, having learned the lesson of Methven, did not attempt to attack the English army but to make small-scale attacks on it, gaining the grudging approval of the cynical cleric who authored the somewhat defamatory *Vita Edwardi Secundi*.

Unable to deal with the Bruce, Edward and Gaveston returned to England to face a host of complaints about their erratic behaviour. Gaveston was exiled to Ireland, then recalled by Edward, and once again the kingdom seemed to be faced with civil war. This time, however, many of the men of the time had simply had enough of the behaviour of their volatile monarch. In 1312, Gaveston and the king found themselves in York, with most of the English baronage at their throats. The pair of them fled to Scarborough, leaving behind their servants and Queen Isabelle. As the queen was three months pregnant at this time, this desertion by her lord and master must have enraged and appalled her. Not altogether surprisingly, she wrote to her brother, the king of the Franks, bitterly complaining of her treatment by her husband.

The Gaveston problem was ended in June 1312. Gaveston, who had been put under the protection of the Earl of Pembroke, was kidnapped by a gang of four other earls, and beheaded near Warwick Castle. His head was presented to the most powerful of the crew, Thomas of Lancaster, who was also the king's cousin. There would be some very interesting later repercussions regarding this incident.

The sight of the leading English nobles at each other's throats was greatly to the advantage of the Bruce. As early as 1311, the Bruce led raids into northern England. For almost twenty years, the northern shires would be held to ransom while their inept leaders fought one another. Led by the Bruce himself, his homicidal brother Edward, his nephew, the arrogant Thomas Randolph, Earl of Moray, and of course by James 'the Black' Douglas (who was regarded as by far the most important of the bunch), the Scots ravaged and raided almost without hindrance. Edward has been bitterly criticised for not doing anything to stop this, and it must be admitted that a lot of this criticism is well founded.

Gaveston's death slowly changed things in England. Some of the earls, shocked by the murder, rallied to Edward. Isabelle, probably relieved that the court favourite had been eliminated, also appears to have come over to her husband's side. And there was now a chance to unify the kingdom with a foreign war, since the situation in Scotland had reached such a pitch that, by June 1314, only the great fortress of Stirling, the port of Berwick, the lands of the pro-English Earl of Dunbar and a few border castles remained in English hands.

The governor of the besieged Stirling Castle, Sir Philip Mowbray (who had nearly killed the Bruce in 1306), made a deal with the Bruce's brother Edward that if the fortress, geographically in the centre of the kingdom, was not relieved by Midsummer Day 1314, it would surrender. This, added to the fact that Edward had promised to help the northern shires, and that the Bruce had declared that any person in exile from Scotland would have their lands forfeited if they did not come and acknowledge him as their king, made the Bannockburn campaign one Edward had to undertake if he did not want to lose all semblance of credibility.

This book will not cover the Bannockburn campaign in detail, but it is well known that a Scottish army, outnumbered almost three to one by the English, defeated their enemy. The Scots were thrust into the streams and marshes of the Forth and the Bannockburn by an army of footmen, marshalled into dense schiltroms or spear rings; the Bruce killed Sir Henry de Bohun, the nephew of the Earl of Hereford, in hand-to-hand combat; and Edward fled the field of battle in total humiliation.

As Aryeh Nusbaacher points out in his study of the battle, *1314 Bannockburn*, the reason for the Scottish victory was not so much the stupidity of the English as the skill and daring of the Bruce. He realised that the English were marching north, thinking the Scots would attack them from that direction, so he boldly attacked from the west, and rolled up the English army into the Bannockburn. In effect, the Bruce did what Frederick the Great would do to the Austrians at Leuthen in 1757 – confusing them as to where his army actually was, and then attacking them from a totally unexpected direction. The end result was that the English army was totally routed; many knights were killed; the castle of Stirling was forced to surrender; and the baggage train captured by the Scottish, according to some historians, gave the Scottish so much booty that the Bruce's monetary problems were solved for years.

It is important to understand Edward's role in the battle; for the most part, he followed the advice of the Earl of Pembroke and his leading barons. The idea that Edward was a military incompetent who lost the battle entirely owing to his own stupidity is unfounded; furthermore, there is no doubt the he fought very bravely, and chroniclers state that he had to be led away by the Earl of Pembroke and Sir Giles de Argentan, smashing away at Scottish foot soldiers with his mace. After he fled the field, Edward rode to Dunbar, then went by ship to Berwick. For the English, the only constructive result of the battle was that he swore if he escaped he would build a Carmelite college. Oriel College in Oxford is the result of this oath.

The defeat at Bannockburn is one of the most catastrophic defeats suffered by the English in their history. It has certainly gone a long way towards shattering the reputation of Edward II, and from this moment on, his reign seems to be (with the exception of one incident) just one long litany of failure and despair.

18

Myton and Boroughbridge: Fiasco and Triumph

Despite defeating the English at Bannockburn, the Bruce, to his great distress, found out that Edward was as obstinate as ever in his claim that he was lord paramount of Scotland. The fact that the Bruce sent Edward his own shield and privy seal that he had lost at the battle, along with a very polite letter suggesting peace would now be the best state of affairs for both kingdoms, seemed to make Edward even more obstinate. The Bruce, who seems to have genuinely wanted peace, had only one choice: to continue the war and start raiding the northern counties of England afresh.

Led, inevitably, by the Douglas, the Scots soon went on the rampage, raiding Westmoreland and reaching as far as Yorkshire. The northern counties despaired of help from Edward and, if they had not been sacked or burned already, paid protection money to the Scots to stop them levelling their properties. One of the reasons why Edward did not do what his subjects expected of him was that, once again, he had managed to make a favourite whom everybody detested, Hugh Despenser. Despenser married one of the sisters of the Earl of Gloucester (who had been most conveniently killed at Bannockburn), seized the richest parts of the Gloucester inheritance (to the fury of other lords in the Welsh March). and, alongside his father, also called Hugh, achieved an ascendancy over the king equal to that of Gaveston. Their predatory habits soon made them – and therefore Edward – hated.

To add to the eternal quarrelling at the English court, Edward's cousin, Thomas of Lancaster, soon made his presence felt. The lord of five earldoms, gained through both inheritance and marriage, Lancaster was easily the most powerful man in the kingdom after Edward. He could have been a moderating force on the king and, as a northerner, could have tried to stop the Scottish raids. Unfortunately for the English kingdom, Lancaster was, if anything, even more stupid, obstinate and lazy than the king. He seems to have had a naturally unpleasant character, and the results of this were felt mostly in the northern counties, which saw their king and the Earl at loggerheads fighting each other, instead of the northern enemy. This complete lack of understanding between the two was largely responsible for the fall of the city of Berwick in 1318, the city that the father of the Douglas had governed with such a lack of distinction.

The fall of this city, the first Scottish town to have fallen to Edward Longshanks, put Edward II in an unbearable position: if he let it go without trying to retake it, then the whole of the northern frontier would be open to assault. If he did try to retake it, he would have to work with his detested cousin. Edward swallowed his pride, made it up with his cousin, agreed some reforms to the royal household, and proceeded to march up to Berwick. As he marched north with the Earls of Lancaster, Pembroke and Hereford and Lords Audley and Damory, he had an army at least 10,000 strong to take the city, the siege of which started on 8 September.

The account of the siege of Berwick is one of the most vivid chapters of Barbour's *The Brut*. He describes the way the English besieged the city, the furious assaults made against the walls, the desperate fighting along the parapet, with fire arrows and gunstones being launched against the town. He tells of how the soldiers in Berwick fought desperately, with the women and children helping the towns-people and soldiers to repel the attackers. (With typical chivalrous blindness, he attributes the bravery of these women and children to the feelings they had for their king and lord, Walter Stewart, not to the terror they felt at the prospect of a successful assault.)

The Bruce was now faced with a situation as dangerous as Bannockburn: if he did not attack the army of Edward, there was a good chance that Berwick, the key to the south-east, would fall. If this occurred, the south of Scotland would once again be open to attack, and the Bruce would again have to go through the miserable process of asking his bruised and battered people to see their lands ravaged; if he did attack, it would be against an army that was, numerically, far superior to his. He decided on the classic move of a guerrilla leader: he would send a raiding party past Edward's army to ravage the lands to the south, and wreck the English army's line of communications.

It was at this point that the Bruce's two most lethal hitmen, the 'Good Sir James Douglas' (the Black Douglas to the English), and the Bruce's arrogant nephew Thomas, Earl of Moray, received orders to ride south and cause mayhem in the land of the Sassenach. The scene was set for the most ludicrous and tragic 'battle' ever to be fought in the county of Yorkshire.

19

'Slain by the Sword, Slain by the Waters': The Chapter of Myton

The Bruce must have formulated his plans quite early, since it is known that the Douglas and Moray were raiding to the north of England as early as 3 March. This time they were not accompanied by the Bruce's brother Edward, who had tried to become king of Ireland in 1315, and had been killed – and his body (of course) quartered – after the battle of Dundalk in 1318.

Taking into account the fact that the Bruce made no attempt to approach Berwick, we must conclude that the army under the Douglas, who was probably the *de facto* commander, numbered over 1,000 men, most of whom would have been mounted. The Scottish swept south down the Vale of York, which has seen so many armies march over its roads. Their passage was marked by the usual ravaging of the villages along the way. North Otterington, Thornton-on-the-Moor and Thornton-le-Street were among the villages in north Yorkshire that suffered at the hands of the hooligans from north of the border.

The author of the *Vita Edwardi Secundi*, the official but somewhat critical life of Edward II, says that a Scottish spy was captured in York around this time, and that this spy told the somewhat disconcerted citizens and the Archbishop of York, William Melton, that the

Douglas and his men were planning to raid to the south, to York, in order to capture Queen Isabelle, who was now staying in that city. The spy offered to be put to death if the story was untrue.

This story, it should be pointed out, is only mentioned in the *Vita*; it does not appear in Barbour's *Brut*, while the *Lanercost Chronicle*, which explains in some detail what happened next, does not describe this incident either. It appears to be rather too strange to be believed. How on earth could the Scottish hope to capture the queen, residing in one of the greatest cities of the realm? How could one of the Douglas's men find his way south to take up residence in York, where his accent and origins would be so obvious? Perhaps the story of the spy is a little ruse to shift the blame of what happened next from the shoulders of Archbishop Melton onto those of the cunning Scots, in much the same way that the German army, after the First World War, tried to explain away their military defeat as the result of a non-existent 'stab in the back' by their politicians.

The Archbishop and the council of York would not really have needed a spy to tell them what was going on in the hinterland of their city. Taking into account that York would have received abundant news from the refugees who were now probably crowding into the city, and that the smoke from villages put to the torch would have been seen quite clearly from the town walls, the Archbishop and his advisers would have been in no doubt at all that the Scottish were approaching. The queen was hurriedly sent by ship to Nottingham on the River Ouse, while the council debated on what to do next.

Against an army of at least 1,000 men, led by one of the most ruthless and able captains of the day, the Archbishop of York decided to mobilise a scratch force. He proceeded to gather a crowd of untrained peasants, farmers, mechanics, merchants and clerics and, according to one enthusiastic chronicler, he led them out against the Scots 'like a second Thurstan' (Thurstan was the Archbishop of York present at the battle of the Standard, who had had the sense to leave the fighting to the professionals). Along with the Archbishop went the Mayor of York, the Chancellor of the Kingdom, John de

Hothum, the Bishop of Ely, and the king's personal notary, Andrew Tang. To ensure that the 'army' had a lot of spiritual backing, a great number of priests, benefited and mendicant, went with this mob, presumably to try to convert the heathen from north of the border.

According to the Lanercost chronicler, the mob marched north-west 'as men unskilled in War, they all marched scattered through the fields and in no kind of array'. At about midday on 20 September, they found themselves advancing towards Myton, a small town on the River Swale beyond which the Scots lay encamped. What the Douglas and Moray must have thought at the sight of this rabble approaching them is not difficult to imagine. According to the *Vita*, the Scots said to themselves: 'these are not soldiers but huntsmen, and will not achieve much'. Their words were all too true.

It appears that the cheerful mob from York advanced in no sort of order whatsoever towards the village of Myton and proceeded to cross over the river, the Scottish watching them, no doubt, with the eye of a shark deciding how to attack its next victim. According to the *Vita*, the Scottish, with their usual diabolical guile, waited on the far bank of the river and fired a large amount of hay. This fourteenth-century smoke screen seemed to work quite well, since when the English 'army' crossed the river they found not an army in full flight, but the Scottish formed up in full schiltrom formation, advancing towards them. (It should be pointed out that the smoke screen is not mentioned by either Barbour or the Lanercost chronicler, while Barbour states that the Scots were drawn up in two formations, not one.)

The ragbag army of the Archbishop of York found themselves facing the most able warriors of the time, who promptly showed their superior training and discipline by emitting a terrific shout, and advanced to the slaughter. Both the *Vita* and the *Lanercost Chronicle* agree that on seeing and hearing the Scottish host, many of the English – unchivalrously but wisely – took to their heels; those who remained were promptly attacked by the Scots and slaughtered. It appears that a large number of these unfortunates had crossed the river, since the *Lanercost Chronicle* mentions that the waters of the Swale claimed the lives of almost a thousand people, and that deaths by the sword numbered about 4,000. Among the dead were the Mayor of York and many of those bellicose clerics whom the Scottish, with typical vulgarity, called 'the Chapter of Myton'.

What we can gather about this fiasco/tragedy is that the English crossed the river in strength to be attacked by the Scots, who managed to cut off those with the bad luck to be on the north bank of the river, and drive them like lemmings into the waters of the Swale. According to the Lanercost chronicler, the Scottish mounted their horses and pursued the English force for several miles; many of them wisely surrendered to the Scots, who took them off for ransom. Among the prisoners taken were William Ayreminne, the Keeper of the King's Rolls, and Andrew Tang, the king's notary, which just goes to show that those who write about war and fighting are best to keep away from it. The Douglas and Moray, after ravaging the area, swept southwards, sacked Boroughbridge and eventually arrived at Castleford on the Aire, the most southerly point reached by the Scots in the Wars of Independence.

As ridiculous as it may seem, the incident at Myton, when reported to the king at Berwick, caused the divisions among the English lords that the Bruce had hoped for. The lords of the south wished to continue with the siege of Berwick, which had nearly been taken in one desperate assault; the lords of the north, however, urged that the siege be broken off so they could march down and defend their lands in Yorkshire. To the fury of the king, at a meeting with his nobles Lancaster urged the army to retreat, and as his men made up about one third of the size of the entire force, Edward had no choice but to disband the army. It appears that he marched south by way of the East March, while the Earl of Lancaster returned via the West March. The Douglas proceeded to outfox both of them, slipping in between them and proceeding back to Scotland, sacking almost every village he passed through.

The author of the *Vita*, who must have been comfortably removed from the fighting, berates the Earl of Lancaster for leaving the siege of Berwick with the city untaken after such a great deal of effort had been put into mounting it. He appears to believe that Lancaster had taken a huge bribe from the Scots, and in page after page he casts doubt on the Earl's honour and honesty. Lancaster was aggrieved at this, and offered to prove his innocence by way of compurgation (a joint oath taken by him and his peers). This was done, although apparently Edward would have liked the Earl to have undergone the test of holding a white-hot iron, to see if the wound blistered, a sure sign of perjury.

The raising of the siege of Berwick and the defeat at Myton were not the only humiliations suffered by the English this year, since in November the heavenly twins Douglas and Moray invaded England through the East March, and ravaged the area so thoroughly that Edward swallowed his pride again, asking for and receiving a two-year truce. He needed this time, since he had managed, with his usual ability to make enemies, to set most of the English establishment at each other's throats.

The reason for this, inevitably, was Edward's choice of favourites, the Despensers. Whether there was a homosexual liaison between the younger Despenser and Edward is not known. What is known is that the two of them, especially the younger, grabbed at any position of patronage that came to hand; the authors of both the *Vita* and the *Lanercost Chronicle* had nothing but abuse for him. The extension of the power of the younger Despenser, following his marriage to the Earl of Gloucester's sister, inevitably caused chaos and, to judge by the remarks made in the *Vita*, Despenser the younger behaved as if he himself were the king, seizing lands, hanging rebels and doing all those things which so delight the readers of the medieval chronicles but which caused such despair to law-abiding persons of the time.

The behaviour of the Despensers created such anger that a revolt of the Welsh Marcher Lords broke out (according to the gossipy but usually well-informed *Lancercost Chronicle*, the Earl of Lancaster was the unseen hand behind this). The Despensers' lands were rav-aged, and it appeared that civil war was about to commence. Edward, showing a decisiveness that should have been used for better pur-poses, had the castles of the south put in order and sent a knight, one Bartholomew Badelsmere, to negotiate with the rebels. This char-acter did himself no favours when, to Edward's fury, he defected to the rebels – a move that was to have interesting consequences several months later.

The rebels moved in force to London, where Edward, once again on the rack for his habit of supporting totally inappropriate favou-rites, swallowed his pride and sent the Despensers into exile, on the advice of the Earl of Pembroke. The father went to France, probably pleased to have escaped; the son, just to show how obtuse or arrogant he was, set himself up as a pirate in the Straits of Dover. It appeared that Edward was now, once again, down and out. However, a most remarkable change was about to take place.

In October, Queen Isabelle went on a pilgrimage to Canterbury. On her return to London, she decided to stay the night at Leeds Castle, which was part of the property of the queens of England. It was governed by Bartholomew Badelsmere who, interestingly, was absent at the time. The queen, not unnaturally, demanded admittance; to her fury, Lady Badelsmere, panicking in her husband's absence, refused.

The queen ordered her attendants to storm the castle and saw them repulsed, with several fatal casualties. This insult could not be ignored. Within a suspiciously brief period of time, the king had managed to gather five of his earls and some troops from the city of London to besiege the place. It was rumoured that Edward was responsible for putting the Badelsmeres in an impossible position by sending the queen on this errand. Some have even suggested it might have been the queen who suggested the adoption of this approach. Be that as it may, the castle was besieged in late October. The Lords of the March, seeing the recrudescence of the king's power, advanced with their troops to Kingston-on-Thames, but found out that they would get no help from the Earl of Lancaster, who was furious with Badelsmere for having acquired lands and titles he thought were his by right.

After Leeds Castle was besieged, Edward for once in his life used his common sense; he ordered his army to march against the Marcher Lords, to revenge himself on them for forcing him to banish the Despensers. By the end of December he was at Cirencester, and proceeded to march north, taking castles at a rate of knots. The Marcher Lords, in despair, sent to Lancaster for help and got none, since Lancaster was now dealing in an undoubtedly treacherous manner with the Scots. Why he tried to communicate secretly with the Scots has been beyond the ken of most historians, as they proceeded to ravage the lands of the north, reaching as far as Richmond in Yorkshire. Many northern knights went to Lancaster to beg help against the Scots, but got the reply that he could do nothing to help them while his king was trying to attack him, an answer that would have been more convincing if he had actually gone south and faced the king, now moving his troops up to the Trent.

In early February, as Edward was advancing upon his lethargic cousin, he received a visit from a northern knight, Andrew Harclay, the Sheriff of Cumberland. Harclay was the only man to defeat the Bruce in any form of combat after 1308, when in 1315, as governor of Carlisle, he had repulsed every assault the Bruce had made on the city. He now begged Edward to come north and repulse the Scots. Edward gave the unhelpful but unfortunately accurate reply that he could do nothing as long as his realm was in revolt against him, and ordered Harclay to come south and help him fight his cousin – whom Edward correctly saw as the moving force behind the revolt. Harclay rode off to the West March, while Edward advanced to the Trent.

Lancaster, joined by some of the Marcher Lords, including the Earl of Hereford, faced the king over the river at Burton-upon-Trent. Edward proceeded to turn his position by marching upstream, sending Lancaster and his men hastily back north to Pontefract. On

the Scottish frontier, Moray and the Douglas, who had been await-
ing a summons from Lancaster (this traitor earl had corresponded
with them under the hilariously inappropriate *nom de plume* 'King
Arthur'), found that for once someone on the English side had managed to trump their efforts. Having marched north from Pontefract
to Boroughbridge, which he reached on the night of 15 March,
Lancaster found himself facing the governor of Carlisle, Harclay.

Whatever he thought of his king's abilities or judgement, Harclay
obviously believed that it was more important to deal with Lancaster
than with the Scots, who had now returned north of the border.
According to the *Vita*, he marched to Boroughbridge at the head of
4,000 men drawn from the West March; he arrived on the evening
of 15 March and occupied the bridge running over the river Ure and
the ford a little to the east of it. It appears that his army consisted of
both men-at-arms and a substantial force of archers. He deployed
them in a very interesting way: it appears that he dismounted his
men-at-arms at both the ford and the bridge and placed them in the
centre of each formation. He placed his archers on the flanks of these
men, adopting a formation that would be used with remarkable success by the English in the wars in France, later in the century.

Lancaster and his reluctant allies must have been appalled at the
sight, since they of course were not expecting Harclay's presence.
The plan they adopted was the only one possible. Lancaster decided
to launch a mounted attack on the ford to the east of Boroughbridge,
while Hereford and his men would attack the bridge. The river
would at this time have been almost in full flood with the meltwater
streams from the Pennines, and anyone who has seen its width will
understand the predicament of the two earls, whose forces were estimated as less than 1,000 strong. Lancaster had ordered his favourite
knight and thug, Thomas Holland, to come to his aid, but Holland,
seeing how the wind was blowing, behaved like any true knight and
swapped over to Edward's side with his men.

The two sides met on 16 March. Hereford and Lord Clifford –
who was the son, ironically, of the man who had been given the

castle of the Douglas – attacked the bridge. We are told that it was so narrow that they could not attack on horseback. Hereford, Clifford and Hereford's standard-bearer, Sir Ralph de Applinsdene, with their reluctant entourage behind them, attacked with a vigour worthy of a better occasion. They were met with a storm of arrows. Hereford, leading the assault, was eviscerated by a Welsh spearman who, distressingly ignorant of the laws of chivalry, was in hiding under the north end of the bridge. Applinsdene was also killed and Clifford was wounded. The rest of the attackers on the bridge retreated. This marked the end of the attack here.

At the ford, or that part of the torrent where the ford was supposed to be, Lancaster led his horsemen. In the vivid words of the *Vita*, as soon as they got within range they 'were most lamentably cut up by a storm of arrows'. Lancaster retreated in confusion. This, in effect, marked the end of the battle of Boroughbridge. Lancaster could think of nothing more than to call a truce, which Harclay, who had all the aces of the pack in his hands, willingly agreed to.

Why Lancaster did not try to take flight has bemused many historians. He, Clifford and his other nobles appear to have gone to their lodgings to stay there for the night. Seeing the way the wind was blowing, their men deserted, having no wish to prove their loyalty to their lords at the end of the hangman's rope. In the early morning, assisted by the Sheriff of York who had come in for the kill, Harclay advanced into the town of Boroughbridge and captured the rebel leaders.

The next few days must have brought great joy to Edward. Lancaster, his bugbear and the killer of Gaveston, was led to his own stronghold of Pontefract, where he was put on trial for his life. His judges were the Earls of Pembroke and Richmond, together with the Despensers father and son, whom Edward, with his usual lack of foresight, had managed to bring home. Forbidden to speak in his own defence, Lancaster was found guilty of treason and sentenced to be hanged, drawn and quartered. Due to his rank, only the third part of the sentence was carried out. Lancaster was led out to be mounted on a mule, where, to add insult to injury, he was paraded around the area and pelted with snowballs by his tenants, who were even more pleased than Edward at the turn of events, as Lancaster was known as a viciously rapacious landlord. The Earl was taken to a nearby hillock, made to face north, in the direction of Scotland, and then, 'like any thief or vilest rascal', was beheaded. To add injury to insult, three strokes of the axe were needed to part the foolish head from the shoulders.

The vengeance of the king did not stop there: numerous knights taken at Boroughbridge, most of whom had only gone to Lancaster in order to secure his help against the Scots, were taken to York and executed. Clifford, whose father had been killed at Bannockburn and whose grandfather drowned while fighting the Welsh in the time of Edward Longshanks, became the third member of his family to die an unnatural death. Thomas Holland, whose desertion of his lord did him little good, was beheaded in Harrow in 1328, in rather vague circumstances. Bartholomew Badelsmere, whose actions were partly responsible for this state of affairs, was taken to Canterbury and hanged.

For once in his life, Edward could be said to be riding high. He decided to take advantage of this situation by making an attack on the Scots which he hoped would be the last. The force he gathered for this attack was by all accounts huge. At least 20,000 men were ordered for the muster at Newcastle, an army greater than that Edward had led at Bannockburn. The Bruce, however, had anticipated this action. He led his troops over the West March, and ransacked the oft-ravaged area of Carlisle and Lancaster. Emboldened by this success, he proceeded to ride as far south as Preston, where a less fortunate army of Scots would come to grief in 1649, fighting against Cromwell.

Having got their blow in first, the Scots retreated into the Lothian, where they prepared to give Edward one shock after another.

20

Byland: Zenith and Nadir

The massive army of the sixth Plantagenet king marched north in early August. Like Napoleon in 1812, they met an enemy who refused to fight: the Bruce had given careful instructions that the inhabitants of the Lothian were to evacuate their lands and leave nothing for the invading English. Edward had made thorough preparations for this campaign, but he must have been astonished at the desert he was marching through. To make things worse, the supply ships, which were so necessary for every English invasion of the lands of the Scots (right up to that of the Duke of Cumberland in 1746), proved to be useless, as Scottish privateers and contrary winds left them either sunk or stranded. The English army, therefore, marched disconsolately and hungrily as far north as Musselburgh, near Edinburgh, where the army halted.

Foraging parties were sent out, one of which managed to bring in a strange catch: one lame cow. The Earl of Surrey remarked sourly that: 'It was the dearest beef he had ever seen, it cost a thousand pound and more.' Frustrated that – once again – he was unable to corner the Bruce, who probably had taken his army north of the Forth, Edward led his army south. According to the Lanercost chronicler, both starvation and dysentery affected the army. When they marched back to England, it must have resembled the retreat of Napoleon from Moscow.

The Bruce now realised he had an opportunity for which he had been waiting years. He could launch an attack on the English, who were now in a sadly weakened state, perhaps capture an important member of the royal government – even Edward himself – and force a peace on them. His actions over the next few weeks represent the apogee of his skills as a general.

As Edward led his army, now in a state of near collapse, back onto English soil, the Bruce followed – then moved south-west to Carlisle. Why he did not attack Edward on the retreat from Scotland has been debated for years. Perhaps he thought the army of the invader still too strong to attack, and wished to let hunger and disease decimate their ranks; perhaps the area over which he would have led his troops was too badly ravaged to give him any sustenance. What is certain is that Edward returned to England and by 26 September had taken up accommodation in Durham. The Bruce led his forces over the West March to Carlisle on 30 September.

There he stayed for five days, contentedly ravaging the lands around the city that had repulsed him in 1315. It appears that he was kept fully informed of the state of Edward's army and the size of his immediate entourage by spies and his border troopers. It was while Edward was at Barnard Castle, on 2 October, that he became aware of the Scots' presence at Carlisle. He ordered that the local magnates and Sir Andrew Harclay, now promoted by a grateful Edward to the earldom of Carlisle, meet him at 'Blackehamour', on the Cleveland hills to the south, which seems to suggest that he did not think the Scots were anything more than a raiding party. That he was ordering a muster also shows that only his court entourage and some local knights must now have attended Edward. This must have been the reason why the Bruce acted as he did.

On or a little after 5 October, the Bruce called the whole of his army together and proceeded to march south-east, up the Eden valley and through the Aire gap. By 13 October the Scots were at Northallerton, the place were David I had such a nasty shock in 1138. The Scots had marched nearly 100 miles in eight days, and Edward, who was ten miles east of Thirsk at Rievaulx, realised with a shock that he was now the hunted.

The speed of the Scottish advance in this and earlier campaigns had always startled the English. This was due to the way that the Bruce and his followers had been forced to fight, as raiders and guerrillas. Their mode of travel is described by one John le Bel, who would take part in a disastrous campaign against them in 1328:

> These Scots are exceedingly hardy. They ride on sturdy horse and bring no wagons with them. They need neither pots nor pans for whenever they invade they find plenty of cattle on use the hides of these in which to boil the flesh. Each man carries an iron place and a little bag of oatmeal. When they have eaten the stewed meat they place the plate on the fire and spread on it a little paste made of oatmeal and water and make a cake in the manner of a biscuit which they eat to comfort their stomachs.

This rather Spartan and basic campaigning style was not playing according to the rules – at least not for fourteenth-century nobles, who entertained no romantic nonsense about sharing hardships with their men, or sleeping under the stars.

On the evening of 13 October, Edward frantically sent out orders to his nobles to assemble their men at Blakehoumor, an action that shows once again that Edward did not have any army with him, only a small escort and his household attendants. Taking into account what followed, the size of the English army that fought the Scots cannot be estimated at more than 1,000 men and was probably much smaller: perhaps only about 500 men.

The Bruce, who seems to have been very well served by his scouts, marched down the great north road from Northallerton on Friday 14 October, to find himself due west of the modern road, which climbs the summit by means of an alarming series of hairpin bends. The numbers of the Scottish army are not known, but they must have easily outnumbered the English. Besides the Bruce, the Scottish leaders included the inevitable Douglas, the Earl of Moray, Walter the Stewart, the Bruce's son-in-law, and the Bruce's standard-bearer,

Gilbert de la Hay. The only member of the Bruce's military 'family' not present was his brother Edward, whose quarters were rotting in various corners of Ireland.

The chroniclers mention the fact that the Bruce was accompanied on this particular march by many Highlanders from the Western Isles, Bute and Arran. It appears that the Bruce had called up almost all of the levies of the kingdom, so we can guess that the Scottish army numbered at least 4,000 men, all of whom had fought together for years, had 'gelled' with each other, and who were now cock-a-hoop with confidence and the expectation of victory. The boldness of the Bruce's march from Carlisle, and his decision to march south from Northallerton immediately on hearing of Edward's presence at Rievaulx, can only be equalled in the history of medieval English warfare by the marches of Edward I in the campaign against de Montfort in 1265, and only surpassed by the march to Stamford Bridge by the great Saxon king, Harold II, in 1066.

The Bruce found himself about six miles away from Edward at Rievaulx, while (according to the Lanercost chronicler) Edward's nephew, John of Brittany, was sent to oppose him at Byland, on the ridge of the Hambleton Hills. Because Edward was at Rievaulx and his troops were at Byland, it has been suggested that Edward was a coward and did not want to take part in the forthcoming battle. There is, however, another possible reason: the speed of the Scottish advance, and the fact that the English were overwhelmingly outnumbered, made them realise they were going to lose. John of Brittany and the 'army' were sent to face the Bruce, in order to give Edward time to escape. This appears to be the best explanation of what followed. It should also be pointed out that, whatever Edward's faults, he was certainly no coward, having fought bravely and most likely killed at Bannockburn.

The Bruce, therefore, found himself at the bottom of the ridge below the position held by Brittany. He devised a plan which, given the exigencies of the situation, was the only one possible: a frontal assault would be launched on the English position while the

Highlanders were directed to clamber up the ridge and assail the English flanks. If all went according to plan, the attack would smash the English force, leaving the Stewart, in command of the Scottish cavalry, to race up the hill, ride on to Rievaulx, and seize Edward.

The Douglas was given the task of leading the attack. Moray, not wanting to be left behind, casually walked over with three of his squires and took up a position behind the Douglas on the front rank, a piece of patrician queue-jumping which would have been more admired then than now. The heavenly twins led the men of the Scottish Borders in their assault on the English position. The English threw a hail of stones at the oncoming Scots, and launched arrows at them. Two knights, Thomas Ughtred and Ralph Cobham, led the English force, and a furious battle soon raged on top of the ridge. Cobham, judged to be one of the best knights in England, was put to flight, and Ughtred was captured. The fighting soon ceased, however, when the Highlanders reached the crest of the ridge and, perhaps led by the Bruce himself, assailed the English force in the flank. The English force crumpled, and the Scots surged forward. The *Lanercost Chronicle*, with all the bitterness of a bloody-minded non-combatant, says that many English escaped by flight. The Scottish cavalry, led by the Stewart, raced past the remnants of the battle and rode east in Edward's direction.

The Scots reached Rievaulx and found no sign of Edward – prudently, he had set off to the east almost as soon as the battle commenced. He left behind him his plate, a group of French knights, led by one Henry de Sully, on a diplomatic mission from the king of France, his treasure, and his privy seal, captured for a second time by the Scots. Once again, the Bruce had the courtesy to send it back to Edward.

The numbers killed at Byland were not in the region of those killed at Bannockburn, but the humiliation was even greater. Bannockburn had been lost in the land of the Scots to the north; Byland had been fought in the middle of Edward's own kingdom. 'Chicken-hearted and luckless in war' was the savage description of Edward by the

Lanercost Chronicle. 'What greater shame could befall the English, that their king should be hunted from place to place by the Scots', cried the Bridlington chronicler. The monks of Bridlington had first realised the outcome of the battle when Edward himself rode up and told them about it. Their shock at seeing their anointed king galloping away in defeat was changed to outrage at his cowardice, especially when the Scots rode up to the monastery and demanded bread and wine, or else…

The battle of Byland, although only a small affair (the *Lanercost Chronicle* gives two full pages to the description of the battle of Bannockburn, about thirty-five lines to the battle of Boroughbridge, and twelve to the battle of Byland), showed the Bruce's skill as a general in both strategy and tactics. The way he waited for the English army to melt away before him, after the failure of the invasion of Scotland in 1322, showed him to be a prudent and careful strategist. The ride from Carlisle to Northallerton, covering 100 miles in less than ten days, was a bold and shrewd manoeuvre, while the march to Northallerton and the decision to attack Edward on the same day were the actions of a general who knew what sort of an army he had under his control, and knew how best to use it. Scotland in the Middle Ages never produced a greater warrior, and Byland was his apogee as a general.

Postscript

Byland forced Edward to the negotiating table, and a truce was signed for thirteen years. Events in England in 1326 forced the Bruce to ignore this truce, and more raiding took place. In a campaign in 1327, described as one of the worst fiascos in English history, the Douglas led his opponents a merry dance, sacked most of the north of England and escaped hastily back to Scotland.

Peace and the sovereignty of Scotland were assured in March 1328, when, in the treaties of Northampton and Edinburgh, a peace was signed with the kingdom of England acknowledging the full independence of the Scottish realm. The work of the Wallace, the Bruce, the Douglas and all the others who helped them was over.

Dramatis Personae

ROBERT THE BRUCE

The Bruce did not live long after the culmination of his life's work. He died, to the grief of the nation and with his friends around him, on 7 June 1329. Only David I proved to be a greater king of the land of the Scots.

EDWARD II

Edward continued to rule, or rather misrule, his kingdom until a revolt, led by his much-misused wife Isabelle and her paramour, Roger Mortimer, led to his deposition in 1327. Nobody raised a finger to save this monarch who, after his favourites the Despensers were executed, was deposed, put in the dungeons of Berkeley Castle, and murdered, some say by means of a red-hot iron inserted in his anus.

JAMES DOUGLAS

After the Bruce died, the Douglas took the Bruce's heart, at the request of the dying king, on a crusade to fight the Moors in Spain. In a battle brought on by the folly of his followers, the Douglas was surrounded. One story says he took off the heart of the Bruce, which he wore round his neck, threw it into the midst of the Moorish army and cried 'Go forward dear heart, at the front where it was thy wont to be'. He then charged into the midst of his enemies, and died fighting to the last. The good Sir James had followed the orders of his liege lord and remained, to the end, a brave and courteous knight.

Bibliography

PRIMARY SOURCES

Barbour, John, *The Brut*. By far the most valuable of the contemporary sources. Barbour was a deacon who wrote in the middle of the fourteenth century; his work is frankly hagiographic, but contains vital evidence about the lives of both the Bruce and the Douglas.

Vita Edwardi Secundi. The official life of Edward II.

The Lanercost Chronicle, edited by W. Stevenson.

The Chronicles of Jean de Froissart. An invaluable guide to how the Scottish fought and marched in the Wars of Independence.

SECONDARY SOURCES

Barrow, G.W.S., *Robert the Bruce and the Community of the Realm of Scotland*.

Bell, G., *Yorkshire Battlefields*.

Bingham, Caroline, *Robert the Bruce*.

Davis, I.M., *The Black Douglas*.

McNamee, Colm, *The Wars of the Bruces*.

Penman, Michael, *The Scottish Civil War*.

Maps and Genealogical Table

The Battle of Byland 1322

The road from Thirsk

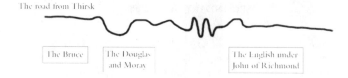

The Bruce

The Douglas
and Moray

The English under
John of Richmond

The Hambleton Hills

———————————→ Route of Edward II to Boroughbridge 1322

·············→ Route of Harclay to Boroughbridge 1322

············→ Route of Edward III to Scotland 1322

———————————→ Route of Edward II and Lancaster to Berwick 1319

············→ Probable route of Douglas and Moray to Myton

ROYAL HOUSE OF SCOTLAND

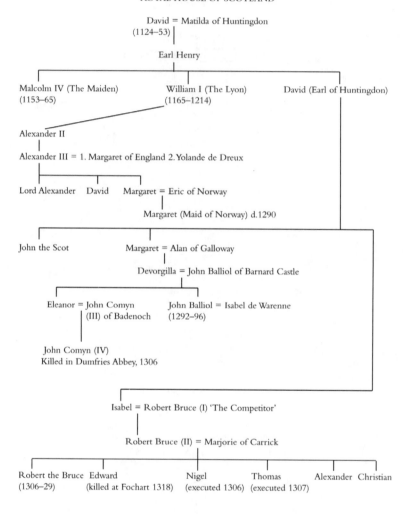

David = Matilda of Huntingdon
(1124–53)

Earl Henry

Malcolm IV (The Maiden)   William I (The Lyon)   David (Earl of Huntingdon)
(1153–65)   (1165–1214)

Alexander II

Alexander III = 1. Margaret of England 2. Yolande de Dreux

Lord Alexander   David   Margaret = Eric of Norway

Margaret (Maid of Norway) d.1290

John the Scot   Margaret = Alan of Galloway

Devorgilla = John Balliol of Barnard Castle

Eleanor = John Comyn   John Balliol = Isabel de Warenne
(III) of Badenoch   (1292–96)

John Comyn (IV)
Killed in Dumfries Abbey, 1306

Isabel = Robert Bruce (I) 'The Competitor'

Robert Bruce (II) = Marjorie of Carrick

Robert the Bruce Edward   Nigel   Thomas   Alexander Christian
(1306–29)   (killed at Fochart 1318) (executed 1306) (executed 1307)

List of Illustrations

Index

TEMPUS REVEALING HISTORY

 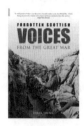  

Scotland From Prehistory to the Present
FIONA WATSON
The Scotsman **Bestseller**
£9.99
0 7524 2591 9

Forgotten Scottish Voices from the Great War
DEREK YOUNG
'A vivid picture of what it was like to be a Scottish soldier in the First World War'
Trevor Royle
£17.99
0 7524 3326 1

Flodden
NIALL BARR
'Tells the story brilliantly' *The Sunday Post*
£9.99
0 7524 2593 5

Scotland's Black Death
The Foul Death of the English
KAREN JILLINGS
'So incongruously enjoyable a read, and so attractively presented by the publishers'
The Scotsman
£14.99
0 7524 2314 2

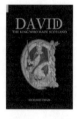  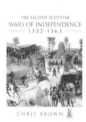 

David I The King Who Made Scotland
RICHARD ORAM
'Enthralling... sets just the right tone as the launch-volume of an important new series of royal biographies' *Magnus Magnusson*
£17.99
0 7524 2825 X

The Kings & Queens of Scotland
RICHARD ORAM
'A serious, readable work that sweeps across a vast historical landscape' *The Daily Mail*
£20
0 7524 2971 X

The Second Scottish War of Independence
1332–1363
CHRIS BROWN
'Explodes the myth of the invincible Bruces... lucid and highly readable' *History Scotland*
£16.99
0 7524 2312 6

Robert the Bruce: A Life Chronicled
CHRIS BROWN
'A masterpiece of research'
The Scots Magazine
£30
0 7524 2575 7

If you are interested in purchasing other books published by Tempus, or in case you have difficulty finding any Tempus books in your local bookshop, you can also place orders directly through our website

www.tempus-publishing.com